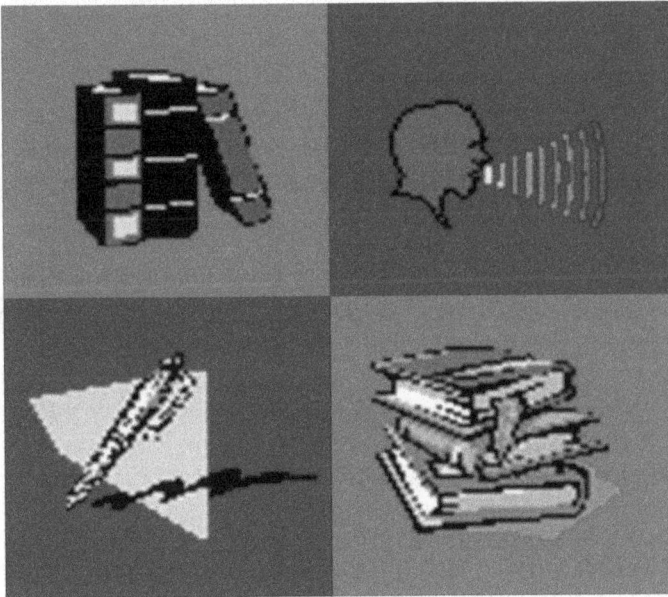

Sybrina's Phrase Thesaurus
Volume 2
Moving Parts – Part 2

By Sybrina Durant

Sybrina's Phrase Thesaurus Book – Volume 2
Moving Parts – Part 2

©1999 & 2013

Volume 1 - Moving Parts – Part 1 – Create Space Print ISBN # ISBN-13: 978-1480083189 & ISBN-10: 1480083186. Lightning Source Print ISBN# ISBN-13: 978-0-9729372-8-3 & ISBN-10: 0972937285

Volume 2 - Moving Parts – Part 2 – Create Space Print ISBN # ISBN-13: 978-1481928182 & ISBN-10: 148192818X. Lightning Source Print ISBN# ISBN-13: 978-0-9729372-9-0 & ISBN-10: 0972937293

Volume 3 - Physical Attributes – Create Space Print ISBN # ISBN-13: 978-1481983051 & ISBN-10: 1481983059. Lightning Source Print ISBN# ISBN-13: 978-0-97891572-0-9 & ISBN-10: 0989157202

Volume 4 - Earth Views – Print ISBN # ISBN-13: 978-1481983136 & ISBN-10: 148198313X. Lightning Source Print ISBN# ISBN-13: 978-0-9891572-1-6 & ISBN-10: 0989157210

Other ISBN #'s for Sybrina's Phrase Thesaurus
Ebook - 978-0-9729372-0-7

Contact Sybrina@sybrina.com

Improve your writing skills...Increase your command of the English language with Sybrina's Phrase Thesaurus. If you use a dictionary or thesaurus, you'll love this writer's aid. Tens of thousands of creative phrases...Hundreds of categories to choose from. Excellent writers aid and fun to read, too!

Have you ever hit a brick wall with your writing? Can't always get the creative juices flowing when you need them? Sybrina's Phrase Thesaurus can help you! Wish you had a better way with words? Is English a new language for you? Sybrina's Phrase Thesaurus can help you!

Sybrina's Phrase Thesaurus is a reference tool for anyone with a need to compose unique, descriptive phrases. It's a great tool for creative writers of any genre including students, people just learning English, people wanting to improve their communication skills, artistic professionals like photographers, videographers, models, actors and many others.

Anyone who enjoys reading unique descriptive phrases will love Sybrina's Phrase Thesaurus because it is packed full of descriptive phrases on every subject ...from descriptions of the body, and how it looks, moves and interacts ...to word pictures describing of all types of landscapes, waterscapes and skyscapes.

Just read the phrases and use what you want just as they're written or better yet, read all the suggested phrases in a particular category for inspiration to conquer your writer's block!

Here's how to use it. All of the categories are coded. Just use the index at the back of the book to browse the different categories. Find one you are interested in and use the code to go directly to the group of phrases for that category.

Sybrina's Phrase Thesaurus was first offered for sale, in 1993, in pdf format with a hyperlinked table of contents. The tool is still available at PhraseThesaurus.com. The book has been available, in its entirety, as an Ebook since 2009. The massive size of the book, well over 800 pages, made it financially impossible to offer it in print until the print-on-demand industry became easily available to independent authors and publishers. In order to keep the price of the books in print lower, the book has been split into 4 smaller sections.

The books are sub-titled and described as follows:

Volume 1 - MOVING PARTS – Part 1 - This book encompasses the top half of the body, describing how it moves and functions. Part 1 covers the everything to do with the head, including voluntary and involuntary actions such as listening, blushing breathing, winking, coughing, singing and much more.

Volume 2 - MOVING PARTS – Part 2 - This book encompasses all of the lower body below the neck, describing how it moves and functions. Part 2 covers topics such as shrugging shoulders, reaching out to touch someone, heart beats, shivering, aching bones, stomach churning, hand gestures, posing, sitting, walking, running and much more. The Body In Motion section includes jumping, skipping, turning, sitting down and getting up, bending, stretching, squirming, falling and body in repose. The Daily Activities section includes creative ways to describe eating meals, driving cars, using a telephone, changing clothes and more. The Figures (or Expressions) Of Speech section includes ideas for writing smooth flowing conversations. Much more than just "He said, She said". Finally the Emotions section contains descriptions of emotions. Joy, anger, fear, sadness and many more.

Volume 3 - PHYSICAL ATTRIBUTES – This book encompasses all of the body describing how different parts of the human body look, from head to toe. This book covers topics such as facial shapes and expressions, age and youth. There are descriptions for bald heads and different kinds of hair styles and colors. There are descriptions for skin colors and textures and all kinds of ways to describe eyes, ears, noses and mouths. The rest of the body is described in great detail as well.

Volume 4 - EARTH VIEWS - This book consists of Landscapes (plains, hills, mountains, valleys), Waterscapes (waterfalls, streams, rivers, ponds) and Skyscapes (morning, sunny, cloudy, rain, space, stars) and much more. There is also a section for COLORS with descriptions for all the colors in the rainbow plus other things like metals, shiney, light, dark, day and night.

Enjoy them all!

MOVING PARTS – Part 2

SH
SHOULDERS

SH101 SHOULDERS 101

1. her arm fell away from his shoulders
2. as his broad shoulders disappeared around the corner
3. behind her shoulder
4. covered her shoulders
5. draped it grandly about his naked shoulders
6. her soft ivory shoulders beckoned to him
7. his gaze dropped from her eyes to her shoulders to her breasts
8. his massive shoulders filled the coat he wore
9. looked up at the powerful set of shoulders
10. the rich outlines of his shoulders strained against the fabric
11. upon her shoulders

SH102 SHOULDERS 102 (SHIVERING)

1. his hands on her shoulders sent an involuntary chill through her
2. felt a shiver touch her shoulders
3. felt a shiver run across her shoulders

SH103 SHOULDERS 103 (GESTURING WITH SHOULDER)

1. walked with shoulders drooped, gait slow and unsteady
2. slouching his shoulders
3. planting palms flat against the surface, he exerted full strength, straining muscles on his arms and shoulders
4. hunching his shoulder, he bent his mind to the nub of the argument

5.	hunched over
6.	his shoulders drooped
7.	he pointed over his shoulder
8.	hunching his shoulder, he bent his mind to the nub of the argument
9.	a shrug that indicated boredom
10.	arched eyebrows, hesitant shrug
11.	did another of her shrugs
12.	he moved his shoulders in a shrug of anger
13.	he shrugged matter-of-factly
14.	he shrugged somewhat owlishly
15.	he shrugged
16.	he gave an impatient shrug
17.	he spread his hands regretfully and shrugged
18.	he moved his shoulders in a shrug
19.	he shrugged his shoulders in mock resignation
20.	he shrugged dismissively
21.	shrugged in mock resignation
22.	gave a resigned shrug
23.	shrugged to hide her confusion
24.	managed to shrug
25.	shrugged somewhat fatalistically
26.	signaled with a twitch of shoulder
27.	taking on that "let's be reasonable" slouch
28.	the tiniest resigned shrug
29.	with a little shrug

SH104 SHOULDERS 104 (TOUCHING)

1.	he grabbed her by the shoulders
2.	spinning her around by the shoulders
3.	without warning a hand closed over her right shoulder
4.	shaking her by the shoulder
5.	shaking the fellow back into attention by the shoulders
6.	his hands rested casually on her shoulders, causing her flesh to tingle
7.	his hand remained on her shoulder a moment too long

8. his fingers biting deeply into her shoulder
9. he put his hand on her shoulder in a possessive gesture
10. guided him with a fingertip touch on his shoulder
11. caught him by the shoulder on either side as supports and herders
12. caught at his shoulder in a tight and demanding grip
13. a hand fell on her shoulder
14. a hand descended on his shoulder from behind
15. a hand clutched her shoulder
16. a change in the pressure of his hands on her shoulders
17. catching her shoulders, he turned her over onto her back
18. gently he pulled the et up over her shoulders and tucked it around her
19. was like a trapped animal, her shoulders pressed against the wall
20. patting his shoulder gently
21. he caught her shoulders and propelled her toward the window
22. he caught her shoulders and shook her hard
23. was conscious of his reassuring hand gently squeezing her shoulder
24. he put his hand protectively on her shoulder
25. he caught hold of her shoulders
26. he felt the silky weight of her hair slide over her shoulders onto his face and neck
27. he rubbed the bare skin of her back and shoulders
28. her hair swung around her shoulders and over her pale breasts
29. he laid a tentative hand on her shoulder
30. felt his fingers on her elbow, then an arm was around her shoulders
31. he took her by the shoulders and shook her
32. felt his fingers lightly touch her shoulders
33. he put his hands on her shoulders, drawing her to him
34. he slapped her playfully on the shoulder
35. he took his shoulder and steered him back to the chair
36. his hands were on her shoulders, gently pulling her toward him

37.   he threw his arm around her shoulders roughly
38.   he had his arm protectively around her shoulders
39.   felt her resistance weakening as he moved his hands slowly from her shoulders toward her breasts, massaging them sensuously
40.   clapping him on his shoulders
41.   he rested his hand awkwardly for a moment on her shoulder
42.   he threw a boisterous arm around her shoulder
43.   buried her head in his shoulder
44.   he leaned forward as if to touch her shoulder, but he changed his mind
45.   caressing her shoulders gently as he pressed her against him

SH105 SHOULDERS 105 (SUPPORTING SOMETHING)

1.   hitching her bag higher on her shoulder
2.   with the support of his shoulder
3.   shoulder to shoulder
4.   wondered if his broad shoulders ever tired of the burden he carried
5.   leaned against the taut smoothness of his shoulder
6.   cuddled into his shoulder
7.   buried her burning face against his shoulder
8.   looped it around his shoulder for safe keeping
9.   his head turned on his shoulders
10.   her head fit perfectly in the hollow between his shoulder and neck
11.   he shouldered
12.   bearing across his shoulders the
13.   scooped the strap of her tote bag onto her shoulder
14.   her weight was exhausting him, tearing at the muscles of his arms and shoulders
15.   supporting her weight on his shoulder
16.   was like a trapped animal, her shoulders pressed against the wall
17.   he carried his jacket over his shoulder, his finger hooked through the loop

18.	his head was bend toward her, resting against his own shoulder
19.	held him close, ignoring the stiffness in her shoulders
20.	buried her head in his shoulder
21.	rested her head on his shoulder and sighed unevenly
22.	her head fit perfectly in the hollow between his shoulder and neck

SH106 SHOULDERS 106 (SHOULDER BLADES)

perspiration trickled down between her shoulder-blades

SH107 SHOULDERS 107 (PAIN)

1.	his fingers biting deeply into her shoulder
2.	her back ached between her shoulder blades
3.	his grip on her wrist tightened and pain shot through her shoulder

SH108 SHOULDERS 108 (STRAIGHTENING SHOULDERS)

1.	standing, straightened her shoulders and cleared her throat
2.	stand with shoulders up
3.	swallowed hard and squared her shoulders
4.	straightened to relieve the ache in her shoulders
5.	pulled back his shoulders and lifted his granite jaw
6.	he grinned and straightened his shoulders
7.	he straightened his shoulders
8.	standing, straightened her shoulders and cleared her throat
9.	suddenly he squared his shoulders
10.	straightening his shoulders
11.	pulled back his shoulders and lifted his granite jaw
12.	he grinned and straightened his shoulders

SH109 SHOULDERS 109 (MOVING THE SHOULDERS)

1. pulled away somewhat haughtily from his grasp
2. he started to shrug the heavy garment off his shoulders
3. turned with a quick snap of his thick shoulders
4. tilting her shoulders one way, her hips another
5. signaled with a twitch of shoulder
6. shoulders shook with laughter
7. tossed her hair across her shoulders in a gesture of defiance
8. hunching his shoulder, he bent his mind to the nub of the argument
9. hunched close to
10. hunching forward
11. his sharp shoulder blades shaking with harsh, tearing sobs he could not control
12. his broad shoulders were heaving as he breathed

SH110 SHOULDERS 110 (KISSING SHOULDERS)

1. his kiss seared a path down her neck, her shoulders

SH111 SHOULDERS 111 (LOOKING OVER SHOULDER)

1. caught herself glancing uneasily over her shoulder
2. looking backwards over her shoulder
3. he looked briefly over his shoulder
4. glanced nervously over her shoulder
5. he flung his instructions over his shoulder
6. glanced half fearfully over her shoulder
7. he said over his shoulder
8. he looked longingly over his shoulder
9. he glanced over his shoulder hurriedly
10. glanced apprehensively over her shoulder toward

SH112 SHOULDERS 112 (STRETCHING)

1. straightened to relieve the ache in her shoulders
2. he shifted his shoulders
3. he got up and stretched the ague from his shoulders

SH113 SHOULDERS 113 (USING SHOULDERS)

1. shouldering his way through the crowd
2. put his shoulder to
3. leaning stiffly against
4. he shouldered
5. easing the heavy bag on her shoulder

SH114 SHOULDERS 114 (PROTECTING SHOULDERS)

1. abruptly he threw his mantle around her shoulders
2. pulled a blanket around her shoulders in spite of the hot night

SH115 SHOULDERS 115 (SLOUCHING)

1. taking on that "let's be reasonable" slouch
2. he slouched against the door as he drove
3. his shoulders drooped a little
4. his head sunk between his shoulders
5. his shoulders slumped with despair

SH116 SHOULDERS 116 (FEELING SENSATIONS)

1. feeling the icy drench of perspiration across his shoulders

CS
CHEST

CS101 CHEST 101

1. buried her face against the corded muscles of his chest
2. he looked very powerful, his chest broad and muscular

CS102 CHEST 102 (TIGHTNESS IN CHEST)

1. feeling the tightness of fear close across her chest like an iron band
2. his chest felt tight and his heart was beating with an uneasy, irregular rhythm
3. felt something tighten in her chest, but this time knew it was fear

CS103 CHEST 103 (CHEST EXPANDING)

1. marching away smartly, head high, chest out
2. her chest felt as if it would burst
3. a great exultation filled his chest to bursting

CS104 CHEST 104 (TOUCHING CHEST)

1. dropped her chin on his chest with a sigh of pleasure
2. his naked chest melded to hers
3. her breasts tingled against his hair-roughened chest
4. held her hand to her forehead, her chin almost resting on her chest
5. fell on his chest
6. brushing her fingers across the dark curling hair of his chest
7. he stood, arms folded across his chest

CS105 CHEST 105 (CHEST HAIR)

1. manly wisps of dark hair curled against the "V" of his open shirt
2. his open shirt revealed a muscular chest covered with crisp brown hair
3. her breasts tingled against his hair-roughened chest
4. brushing her fingers across the dark curling hair of his chest

CS106 CHEST 106 (HEAVINESS IN CHEST)

1. the heaviness in her chest felt like a millstone
2. a heaviness centered in her chest

CS107 CHEST 107 (CHEST MOVING)

1. lay panting, her chest heaving
2. pectoral muscles in perfect colloquy with the movement of his arms
3. chest heaving

CS108 CHEST 108 (SUPPORTING SOMETHING)

1. buried her face against the corded muscles of his chest
2. folded her arms across her chest
3. nursing his right hand and arm against his chest
4. held it cupped against his chest
5. dropped her chin on his chest with a sigh of pleasure
6. held her hand to her forehead, her chin almost resting on her chest

CS109 CHEST 109 (CHEST TO CHEST OR BREAST)

1. gasped as bare chest met bare chest
2. felt her breasts crush against the hardness of his chest
3. his naked chest melded to hers
4. gasped as bare chest met bare chest
5. felt her breasts crush against the hardness of his chest
6. his naked chest melded to hers
7. her breasts tingled against his hair-roughened chest

CS110 CHEST 110 (EXPOSING CHEST)

1. he bared his breast
2. pectoral muscles in perfect colloquy with the movement of his arms

3.   manly wisps of dark hair curled against the "V" of his open shift

CS111 CHEST 111 (FEELING SENSATIONS)

passion pounded the blood through her heart, chest, and head

CS112 CHEST 112 (PAIN IN CHEST)

1.   her chest clenched with pain
2.   a hot, pulsing pain filled her chest
3.   a diagonal line of pain cut across her chest, making it impossible to inhale

BS
BREAST

BS101 BREAST 101

1.   the light rippled on her ivory breasts

BS102 BREAST 102 (TOUCHING)

1.   felt his hands closing on her breasts
2.   gently he reached out and touched her breasts
3.   mutely her hands went to her breasts
4.   crossed her arms, trying to ease the discomfort in her breasts
5.   the butterfly play of his fingers searching for her nipples
6.   the soft firmness of one of her breasts just touched the side of his face
7.   gasped as bare chest met bare chest
8.   felt her breasts crush against the hardness of his chest
9.   outlining the tips of her breasts with his fingers
10.   holding him at her nipples, slid partially under him
11.   his hand on her breast continued to move gently

12. his hands roamed intimately over her breasts
13. his palms followed the curves of her breasts
14. his hands roamed over her breasts with lust-arousing exploration
15. his hand lightly touched her hardening nipples
16. his hands moved magically over her smooth breasts
17. her nipples firmed instantly under his touch
18. he fondled the small globe, its pink nipple marble hard
19. gently his hand outlined the circle of her breast
20. fanning his fingers wide apart, he circled her breast
21. a heavy lock of her hair slipped forward onto her breast
22. feeling her body tremble as he reached inside her blouse
23. his tongue explored the rosy peaks of her breasts
24. his mouth left hers and traveled down her throat toward her breasts
25. his mouth closed softly over the flower of her breast
26. his tongue caressed her sensitive swollen nipples
27. his tongue tantalized the buds which had swollen to their fullest
28. lips teased a taut dusky pink nipple
29. his tongue explored the rosy peaks of her breasts
30. lips brush her nipples
31. lips touched her nipple with tantalizing possessiveness
32. he tore her shirt open and dropped his head to nuzzle her breasts
33. a heavy lock of her hair slipped forward onto her breast
34. her hair swung around her shoulders and over her pale breasts
35. his hands crud her breasts before moving on to caress her body
36. his fingers moved forward and down until they closed over her breasts
37. he tore her shirt open and dropped his head to nuzzle her breasts
38. his mouth left hers and traveled down her throat toward her breasts

39.   his hands feeling for her breasts in the low neckline of her
       gown

BS103 BREAST 103 (FEELING SENSATIONS)

1.   her breasts ached
2.   the burning sweetness of her hardened nipples
3.   felt the thundering of his heart pounding against her breasts
4.   felt a deep, unaccustomed pain in her breast
5.   his heart swelled burstingly in his breast
6.   her heart fluttered wildly in her breast
7.   her heart ached under her breast
8.   her breasts firm with aching arousal
9.   her nipples, taut beneath the thin fabric
10.   her breast tingled against the fabric
11.   her nipples were erect from the cold
12.   fire seared through her breast
13.   a stab of guilt lay buried in her breast
14.   could feel the sudden perspiration on her back and between
      her breasts
15.   felt her breasts crush against the hardness of his chest

BS104 BREAST 104 (RESPONDING TO STIMULI)

1.   the rosy peaks grew to pebble hardness
2.   the rose-hued tips were puckered with desire
3.   his hand lightly touched her hardening nipples
4.   her taut nipples strained against the thin fabric
5.   her full young breasts budded with pink
6.   her breasts surged at the intimacy of his touch
7.   her breasts firm with aching arousal
8.   her nipples were erect from the cold
9.   her nipples firmed instantly under his touch
10.   her breasts tingled against his hair-roughened chest
11.   kissed her taut nipples, rousing a melting sweetness within
      her

12.	he fondled the small globe, its pink nipple marble hard
13.	fire seared through her breast
14.	bringing their pink tips to crested peaks
15.	his tongue caressed her sensitive swollen nipples
16.	lips drew her nipple taut

BS105 BREAST 105 (MOVING)

1.	the deep upward and downward heaving of her breasts
2.	the movement of her breast
3.	rise and fall of her breathing
4.	her breasts thrust toward him, firm and full
5.	her breasts rose and fell under her labored breathing

BS106 BREAST 106 (KISSING BREASTS)

1.	he tore her shirt open and dropped his head to nuzzle her breasts
2.	his tongue tantalized the buds which had swollen to their fullest
3.	his mouth closed softly over the flower of her breast
4.	his tongue caressed her sensitive swollen nipples
5.	lips brush her nipples
6.	lips teased a taut dusky pink nipple
7.	lips drew her nipple taut
8.	his tongue explored the rosy peaks of her breasts
9.	lips touched her nipple with tantalizing possessiveness
10.	kissed her taut nipples, rousing a melting sweetness within her
11.	his mouth left hers and traveled down her throat toward her breasts

BS107 BREAST 107 (EXPOSING BREAST)

1.   he tore her shirt open and dropped his head to nuzzle her breasts
2.   he eased the lacy cup of her bra aside
3.   bending forward to get a glimpse of cleavage
4.   her bed-gown had fallen open to reveal her full breasts, half swathed in her long copper hair
5.   he bared his breast
6.   the bodice of her gown falling carelessly loose, showing a heavy brown breast with its broad, reddened nipple

BS108 BREAST 108 (SUPPORTING SOMETHING)

1.   hugging against her bosom

BS109 BREAST 109 (COVERING BREAST)

1.   crossed her hands on her breast
2.   mutely her hands went to her breasts
3.   lifted her arms to cover her breasts

BS110 BREAST 110 (LACTATING)

1.   only the fullness of her breasts betrayed the recent childbirth
2.   a drop of watery blue liquid formed on her left nipple

BS111 BREAST 111 (LOOKING AT BREASTS)

1.   his eyes traveled to her breasts, outlined beneath the low-buttoned blouse
2.   his gaze dropped from her eyes to her shoulders to her breasts

RB
RIBS

RB101 RIBS 101

1. trying to steady the uneasy pounding of the pulse beneath her ribs
2. his tongue made a path down her ribs to her stomach
3. poked at his ribs
4. stood breathing with rib-stretching gasps
5. there was a band of tight, hard pain about his lower ribs
6. felt her heart tighten beneath her ribs

RB102 RIBS 102 (RIBS MOVING)

1. stood breathing with rib-stretching gasps

RB103 RIBS 103 (TOUCHING RIBS)

1. giving him a slight nudge in the ribs

RB104 RIBS 104 (FEELING CONSTRAINED)

1. her heart hammered against her ribs
2. could feel her heart beginning to pump uncomfortably beneath her ribs

LN
LUNGS

LN101 LUNGS 101

1. her lungs were beginning to burn with the need for air
2. the air whistled out of her lungs
3. drew a deep painful breath of air into her lungs
4. good to open up one's lungs and take in whole luscious barrelfuls of air
5. inspire terror through the lungs
6. a prodigious exhalation relieved his lungs
7. howled with all the lungs he had
8. heart jumped up amongst my lungs

9.   heart fell down amongst my lungs
10.   drew into his lungs deep breaths
11.   chanting, at the full stretch of his lungs
12.   exerted all the power of my lungs
13.   the movements of his lungs as he breathed
14.   breathing with what was left of his lungs
15.   air restored the lungs to their normal condition
16.   bellowed with all the power of his lungs
17.   his lungs throbbed suddenly with hope
18.   jerking at each convulsion of his lungs
19.   drawing in the air to the full depth of his lungs
20.   with a great gasp he filled his lungs afresh
21.   coughed his lungs away
22.   his lungs performed their functions freely
23.   lungs began to give way
24.   the lungs expelled the air with rapidly succeeding
      interruptions
25.   striving to get her lungs full
26.   her lungs had a perceptible movement
27.   a perpetual cough tickles my lungs and throat
28.   was troubled with weak lungs
29.   his lungs expanding with long draughts of mountain air
30.   sing with all your lungs

HT
HEART

HT101 HEART 101

1.   her heart whispered back
2.   there were no shadows across her heart

HT102 HEART 102 (BEATING)

1.	her heart beat with the pulse of the music
2.	her heart thudded once, then settled back to its natural rhythm
3.	her heart had begun to beat in a quick, uneasy rhythm
4.	could feel her heart beginning to beat faster as his mouth moved gently against hers
5.	her heart beating with excitement
6.	his heartbeat throbbed against her ear
7.	felt the thundering of his heart pounding against her breasts
8.	her heart was pounding violently
9.	her heart thumping nervously
10.	her heart was beating too quickly

HT103 HEART 103 (ACHING)

1.	her heart ached under her breast
2.	the only things left were the raw sores of an aching heart
3.	the question was a stab in her heart
4.	the pain in her heart became a sick and fiery gnawing
5.	saw the heart rending tenderness of his gaze
6.	her heart squeezed in anguish
7.	her heart ached under her breast
8.	her heart aching with pain
9.	a pain squeezed her heart as thought of him
10.	her heart bursting with love and anguish
11.	felt a rock fall through her heart
12.	felt her heart tighten beneath her ribs

HT104 HEART 104 (JUMPING)

1.	when the air hit her burning lungs, her heart stuttered
2.	her heart fluttered wildly in her breast
3.	his heart bounded into his throat
4.	at the base of her throat a pulse beat and swelled as though her heart had risen from its usual place
5.	his heart bounded into his throat
6.	his heart jumped
7.	his heart gave a great bound

8.   his breath was warm and moist against her face, and her heart raced
9.   her heart lurched madly
10.   her heart jumped in her chest
11.   her heart pounded an erratic rhythm
12.   her heart thudded once, then settled back to its natural rhythm
13.   her heart thumped erratically
14.   her heart fluttered wildly in her breast
15.   her heart took a perilous leap
16.   her heart jolted and her pulse pounded
17.   every time his gaze met hers, her heart turned over in response
18.   her heart leapt
19.   her heart in her mouth

HT105 HEART 105 (POUNDING)

1.   her heart hammered against her ribs
2.   could feel her heart beginning to pump uncomfortably beneath her ribs
3.   felt the thundering of his heart pounding against her breasts
4.   passion pounded the blood through her heart, chest, and head
5.   her breath caught in her throat as felt her heart pounding
6.   the glimpses of his strong gold body made her heart beat more rapidly
7.   stared wordlessly across at him, her heart pounding
8.   set his heart to pounding
9.   passion pounded the blood through her heart, chest and head
10.   his heart beat fast and hard
11.   his heart was hammering
12.   his heart was thudding
13.   her heart was hammering foolishly
14.   her heart began to hammer in her chest
15.   her heart was thumping madly
16.   her heart was thundering
17.   her heart pounded an erratic rhythm
18.   her heart was hammering

19. her heart thudded noisily within her
20. her heart caught in her throat as felt her heart pounding
21. her heart fluttered wildly in her breast
22. her heart hammered against her ribs
23. her heart jolted and her pulse pounded
24. blood pounded in her brain, leapt from her heart, and made her knees tremble
25. trying to steady the uneasy pounding of the pulse beneath her ribs
26. her heart was pounding uncontrollably
27. her breath caught in her throat as felt her heart pounding
28. blood pounded in her brain, leapt from her heart, and made her knees tremble
29. her heart pounding nervously
30. could feel her heart beginning to pump uncomfortably beneath her ribs
31. her heart thumped in her chest
32. her heart suddenly hammering in her chest
33. her heart began to hammer again at the word
34. her heart thumping nervously

HT106 HEART 106 (STOPPING)

1. halting her heart for a beat or two
2. heart stood still for a moment

HT107 HEART 107 (SINKING)

1. her heart went down, it sank, almost literally
2. felt her heart sink, the tears rising unbidden behind her lids
3. her heart growing suddenly cold at his tone

HT108 HEART 108 (RACING)

1. the glimpses of his strong gold body made her heart beat more rapidly
2. his heart beat fast and hard

3.   her heartbeat skyrocketed
4.   her heart danced with excitement
5.   her heart beating wildly
6.   could feel her heart beginning to beat faster as his mouth moved gently against hers
7.   his breath was warm and moist against her face, and her heart raced

HT109 HEART 109 (SWELLING)

1.   his heart swelled burstingly in his breast
2.   her heart seemed to rush to the spot he touched
3.   her heart swelled with a feeling had thought long since dead

HT110 HEART 110 (HEARTFELT JOY)

1.   his heartbeat high
2.   her heart danced with excitement
3.   her heart sang with delight
4.   he had unlocked her heart and soul
5.   a feeling of glorious happiness sprang up in her heart

HT111 HEART 111 (HEART FELT SORROW)

1.   her heart squeezed in anguish
2.   grief and despair tore at her heart
3.   anguish seared her heart
4.   slowly, with a leaden heart, he walked up the passage

HT112 HEART 112 (HARDENING HEART)

1.   tried to keep her heart cold and still
2.   hardening her heart by erecting barriers of anger

HT113 HEART 113 (THINKING WITH THE HEART)

1.   the hunger to leave gnawed in his heart
2.   had walked into it with her heart wide open
3.   her heart refused to believe what her mind told her

HT114 HEART 114 (HEARING HEARTBEATS)

1.   could hear nothing but the wild thumping of her own heart
2.   the noise drowned out the thudding of her heart
3.   her heartbeat throbbed in her ears
4.   her heart hammered in her ears
5.   her wildly beating heart was the only sound audible
6.   her heart thudded noisily within her

HT115 HEART 115 (SKIPPING BEATS)

1.   her heart lurched madly
2.   her heart thudded once, then settled back to its natural rhythm
3.   her heart thumped erratically
4.   her heart jolted and her pulse pounded
5.   felt it jolt her system, making her heart palpitate uncomfortably
6.   his chest felt tight and his heart was beating with an uneasy, irregular rhythm
7.   pressed her hand against her heart, feeling its irregular fluttering

HT116 HEART 116 (HEARTFELT FEAR)

1.   in her heart had always been afraid
2.   icy fear twisted around her heart
3.   felt the cold black shadow of fear hovering over her heart

HT117 HEART 117 (FEELING HEARTBEAT)

1. could feel his heart thudding against her own
2. pressed her hand against her heart, feeling its irregular
    fluttering

HT118 HEART 118 (PASSION)

1. the glimpses of his strong gold body made her heart beat
    more rapidly
2. the fire spread to her heart

HT119 HEART 119 (CALMING)

1. tried to slow his pumping heart
2. the pounding of her heart finally quieted

NV
NERVES

NV101 NERVES 101

1.   with a sudden shot of adrenaline in her stomach realized
2.   was taut as a wire
3.   the soft voice brought her upright with a jerk
4.   panic shot through her
5.   felt her stomach tighten
6.   felt the rags of tension beginning to pull at her temples
7.   the sudden ringing of the phone made her jump
8.   took a deep breath and tried to relax
9.   the voice from the end of the dark room made her jump
     nearly out of her skin
10. felt a tremor of unease

11.	closed her eyes, trying to steady the sudden irrational wave of fear that had filled her
12.	the muscles in her stomach were clenching nervously
13.	felt a prickle of apprehension
14.	he was nervous as a cat
15.	a wave of apprehension swept through her
16.	a strange, cold excitement filled his whole being
17.	a thrill of frightened anticipation touched her spine
18.	a flicker of apprehension coursed through her
19.	alarm and anger rippled along her spine
20.	all her nervousness slipped back to grip her
21.	an animal instinct told him all was not well
22.	anxiety spurted through her
23.	every fiber in her body warned her against him
24.	explosive currents raced through her
25.	he felt a curious, tingling shock
26.	he struck a vibrant chord in her
27.	her insides jangled with excitement
28.	her nerves tensed immediately
29.	his flesh crawled, his instincts warned
30.	his mouth wandered up the tingling cord of her neck
31.	only now that he was gone did dare relax
32.	panic was rioting within her
33.	pulled by the vitality zinging through her
34.	sent a crawling chill up his back
35.	sent waves of excitement through her
36.	fought to keep her fragile control
37.	had to conquer her involuntary reactions to that gentle loving look of his
38.	jumped at the sound of his voice
39.	tingled as he said her name
40.	couldn't help but notice the tingle of excitement inside her
41.	felt a lurch of excitement within her
42.	felt a ripple of excitement
43.	felt a terrible tenseness in her body
44.	felt an electric sparkle, like knowing you're soon to go on holiday

45. felt an unwelcome surge of excitement
46. felt disturbing quakes in her serenity
47. felt her composure was under attack
48. couldn't control the spasmodic trembling within her
49. was actually trembling now
50. was irritated at the thrilling current moving through her
51. was so tired her nerves throbbed
52. was unnerved by the sudden change
53. 'd been more tense than 'd thought
54. er black fright swept through her
55. shock flew through her
56. that sound that could not be heard, only felt with each atom of his tense body
57. the concave hollow of her spine tingled at his touch
58. the tight knot within her begged for release
59. the unwelcome tension stretched ever tighter between them
60. the very air around her seemed electrified
61. the world was filled with a piercing screaming, which tore at his body, cell by living cell
62. warning spasms of alarm erupted within her
63. wave after wave of shock slapped at her
64. recognized her with a violent sense of shock

NV102 NERVES 102 (NERVE ENDINGS)

1. he felt a prickle of unease stir the small hairs at the nape of his neck
2. the touch of lips on hers sent a shock wave through her entire body
3. her skin was drawn tight with fatigue and worry
4. felt a whisper of cold air across her skin
5. the voice from the end of the dark room made her jump nearly out of her skin
6. goose pimples raised on the flesh across his shoulders
7. he could feel the goose bumps rising on his skin
8. he felt the prickle of fear touch the skin at the back of his neck

9. a nervous tic had begun at the corner of his eye
10. the touch of his fingers sent little tingles of excitement up and down her spine
11. little prickles of panic were beginning to chase up and down her back

PL
PULSE

PL101 PULSE 101

1. felt her pulse beat in her throat
2. kissed the pulsing hollow at the base of her throat
3. at the base of her throat a pulse beat and swelled as though her heart had risen from its usual place
4. passion pounded the blood through her heart, chest and head
5. her heart seemed to rush to the spot he touched
6. her heart jolted and her pulse pounded
7. at the base of her throat a pulse beat and swelled as thought her heart had risen from its usual place
8. felt below his ear for his pulse
9. trying to steady the uneasy pounding of the pulse beneath her ribs
10. he could feel a pulse beginning to flicker somewhere in his throat
11. he gave her a smile that sent her pulses racing
12. bit her lip until it throbbed like her pulse
13. the blue veins in her temples beat wildly
14. her insistent voice cut slowly through the pulsing in his head
15. a new and unexpected warmth surged through her
16. a quiver pulsed through her veins
17. a pulsing knot within her demanded more
18. at the base of her throat a pulse beat and swelled as though her heart had risen from its usual place
19. explosive currents raced through her
20. felt it racing through her bloodstream
21. he could feel his panic rising

22. he gave her a smile that sent her pulses racing
23. kissed the pulsing hollow at the base of her throat
24. her blood soared with unbidden memories
25. her pulse quickened at the speculation
26. her pulse skittered alarmingly
27. her pulse began to beat erratically
28. her heart beat with the pulse of the music
29. her heart jolted and her pulse pounded
30. his pulse was racing
31. it sent her pulses spinning
32. it was impossible to steady her erratic pulse
33. waited until her quickened pulse subsided
34. felt the blood surge from her fingertips to her toes
35. bit her lip until it throbbed like her pulse
36. felt her pulses suddenly leap with excitement
37. waited until her quickened pulse had quieted
38. felt her pulse beat in her throat
39. tried to deny the pulsing knot that had formed in her stomach
40. felt blood coursing through her veins like an awakened river
41. knew with pulse-pounding certainty
42. suddenly her blood rose in a jet
43. the beat of the drums became one with his pumping blood
44. the blood began to pound in her temples
45. the answer was a rapid thud of her pulse
46. the muscles rippling under his white shirt quickened her pulse
47. the strange surge of affection felt frightened her
48. they both rose; blood pressure and surface body temperature
49. with a pulse-pounding certainty knew
50. could feel the blood pounding in her temples

BD
BLOOD

BD101 BLOOD 101

1. passion pounded the blood through her heart, chest and head
2. blood pounded in her brain, leapt from her heart, and made her knees tremble
3. there was an angry bloody welt across her back
4. he took a furious swing at the man's face, splitting his lip so the blood spattered across his chin
5. blood pounded in her brain, leapt from her heart, and made her knees tremble
6. could feel the blood pounding in her temples
7. grabbed at the door jamb for support as the blood drained from her head and a strange roaring filled her ears
8. his blood was conscious of a terrible sensation
9. sweating blood for them
10. was in the blood
11. concreted into actual flesh and blood
12. his veins were full of ancestral blood
13. by his gait there was blood in his eye
14. made drunk with blood
15. his veins were full of blood
16. eyes shone with blood
17. put to death in cold blood
18. like hounds to the scent of blood
19. paid the debt of blood by
20. shed my heart's blood for
21. draining my life-blood
22. his head swam, from the rush of blood
23. his blood became calm
24. fever of life in your blood
25. so fair is their complexion that the blood shines through the skin like blue penciling
26. skin of such transparency that the blood shone through it

BD102 BLOOD 102 (TURNING COLD)

1. her blood turned to ice
2. making your blood run cold
3. the warm blood in her body to become cold

4.   the blood left their cheeks
5.   curdling the blood
6.   my blood ran back
7.   frightened the blood from her pale cheeks
8.   curdled the blood in my veins
9.   face grew whiter and whiter, as the blood receded
10.   blood seemed to freeze

BD103 BLOOD 103 (BLEEDING)

1.   something warm and sticky covered his right cheek and temple
2.   blood was spurting out of
3.   the blood was spouting
4.   spilt half an ounce of his blood
5.   weakened by loss of blood
6.   the blood flowed into his eyes, and blinded him for a moment
7.   a small stream of blood was flowing down
8.   the blood and sweat obscured the light from her eyes
9.   blood poured forth in a stream
10.   the blood came trickling down
11.   strove to stanch the blood
12.   the blood could not be stopped
13.   spilling life in streams of dark blood
14.   the darkened blood spouting up through a red gash
15.   streaming with blood
16.   blood issued drop by drop
17.   the blood from the cut stiffening
18.   out of which wound much blood gushed

BD104 BLOOD 104 (HEATING)

1.   the sight of her moved his stagnant blood
2.   felt the blood rush up into her face and tingle in her ears
3.   her cheeks felt heated by beating blood
4.   walking is good to keep the blood stirred up and active
5.   sympathetic blood surged to my temples

6. that made my blood boil
7. warmed all his blood
8. all the blood seemed to rush to her heart
9. set her blood in flame
10. the blood rushed to her heart, and a vivid blush stained her cheeks
11. hot and rebellious liquors in my blood
12. he kept his blood on fire with whiskey
13. in his veins the warm blood swept up
14. blood ran hotly and his pulses were leaping
15. it got into her blood and into her brain like an intoxicant
16. the blood surged to his very brows
17. his blood started with the fancy
18. felt the blood redden his forehead
19. the blood flushed his lips and cheeks brightly
20. a premonition drove the blood to his heart
21. blinding rush of heated blood from heart to brain

VN
VEINS

VN101 VEINS 101

1. sipped her wine, grateful for the warmth it spread through her veins
2. his kiss sang through her veins
3. could feel the heat of the coffee seeping into her veins
4. you've milk in your veins, not blood
5. seem to have their veins filled with milk only
6. lymph in your veins instead of blood
7. veins brimming with blue blood
8. the close netting of the veins is a secondary sexual character in the males
9. the blood of some more humble creature flows in his veins
10. as if his veins would pour out his existence
11. her poor wasted veins

12.   it got into her veins
13.   found rich veins of jealousy

VN102 VEINS 102 (THROBBING)

1.   you could see his arteries throbbing in his neck
2.   sent the tide of life in healthful currents through the veins
3.   the blue veins in her temples beat wildly
4.   passion circulated in my veins
5.   the exhilarating gush of young life shot through their veins
6.   as if her veins ran lightning
7.   fire of passion was still in his veins
8.   the blood in their veins is boiling quicksilver
9.   could see the vein beginning to throb in his neck
10.   a draught from the fast-flowing veins
11.   sent the blood coursing through the veins

VN103 VEINS 103 (BULGING)

1.   could see the vein beginning to throb in his neck
2.   his bulging vein protruded when he did bicep curls
3.   the veins of his forehead swollen with contending passions
4.   the veins stood out at his temples with passion
5.   he had thick veins in his forehead
6.   his veins so much thicker when angry
7.   with the veins in his forehead swelling quickly
8.   passionate veins started out in his forehead
9.   the vein in his forehead swelled like a thick black snake

VN104 VEINS 104 (FEAR)

1.   set the blood rotting in her veins
2.   felt a mortal cold run through all my veins
3.   blood turned like ice in her veins
4.   felt her veins chilled by

5.   it made my blood run cold in my veins

BL
BELLY

BL101 BELLY 101

1.   belly bounced in a chuckle
2.   belly to the ground
3.   he lay belly-flat
4.   the muscles of her thighs and belly flexed rhythmically
5.   turned on her belly
6.   twisted his guts into a knot

BL102 BELLY (TOUCHING)

1.   he put his hand on her belly
2.   a blow in the belly
3.   hands folded on his belly
4.   he pressed her belly hard against his
5.   his hand seared a path down her abdomen and onto her thigh
6.   his hands slid across her silken belly
7.   the kiss sent the pit of her stomach into a wild swirl

ST
STOMACH

ST101 STOMACH 101

ST101 STOMACH 101 (EMOTIONAL REACTIONS)

1.   with a sudden shot of adrenaline in her stomach realized
2.   felt her stomach tighten
3.   a cold knot formed in her stomach

4.   it made her stomach turn over with fear
5.   her stomach turned over in icy shock as recognition his her
6.   her stomach churning with anxiety and frustration
7.   his stomach twisted with the hard knot of need
8.   molten shafts of sensation ran down her stomach to her legs
9.   tried to deny the pulsing knot that had formed in her stomach
10.   felt ice spreading through her stomach

ST102 STOMACH 102 (PHYSICAL SENSATIONS)

1.   in reaction to the cold, her stomach knotted with nausea
2.   her stomach twisted with nausea
3.   felt a muscle somewhere in her stomach start to tense
4.   his stomach heaved and he staggered a couple of paces back, retching into the grass
5.   the muscles in her stomach were clenching nervously
7.   trying to ignore the sudden tightening of her stomach muscles
6.   her stomach muscles knotted
7.   her stomach clenched tight
8.   her stomach knotted
9.   the pit of her stomach churned
8.   there was a heavy feeling in her stomach
9.   there was a tingling in the pit of her stomach
10.   there was a sourness in the pit of her stomach
11.   tried to control his stomach muscles
12.   turned on her stomach
13.   so many drinks on an empty stomach was going to her head

ST103 STOMACH 103 (TOUCHING STOMACH)

1.   held herself upright, holding in her stomach
2.   holding his stomach
3.   one hand slid down her taut stomach to the swell of her hips
4.   he explored her thighs then moved up to her taut stomach
5.   his hands massaging the satiny planes of her stomach
6.   his tongue made a path down her ribs to her stomach

7.   his tongue made a path down her ribs to her stomach
8.   patted her stomach affectionately

BW
BOWELS

BW101 BOWELS 101 (SICK)

1.   in reaction to the cold, her stomach knotted with nausea
2.   her stomach twisted with nausea
3.   he fought back a wave of nausea
4.   felt suddenly overwhelmed with nausea and faintness
5.   his stomach heaved and he staggered a couple of paces back, retching into the grass
6.   swallowed hard, trying to control the urge to retch
7.   a sensation of intense sickness and desolation swept over her
8.   a shaft of pain swept through his bowels
9.   again was assaulted by her sick yearning
10.   deep sobs racked her insides
11.   fear and anger knotted inside her
12.   it was senselessly and sickeningly familiar
13.   one hand pressed to his heaving middle
14.   pain ripped through his insides
15.   relieved himself
16.   felt a nauseating sinking of despair
17.   felt a curious swooping pull at her innards
18.   stunned and sickened, repeated what he said
19.   the thought tore at her insides
20.   the kiss sent the pit of her stomach into a wild swirl
21.   the pit of her stomach churned
22.   there was a sourness in the pit of her stomach
23.   a wave of nausea shook him
24.   he felt suddenly violently sick

HG
HUNGER

1. it was devoured in hungry bites
2. hungry and faint
3. she had never been quite so hungry before
4. I'm so hungry now that I could almost eat you
5. she had naturally begun to be hungry again before evening
6. staring me in the face like a hungry dog
7. as hungry as so many hawks
8. as hungry wolves, with raging appetites
9. he ate greedily, for he was very hungry
10. so hungry he couldn't eat politely
11. I ain't bread and butter hungry, I'm plum cake hungry.
12. were hungry enough to do justice to any fare
13. not half as hungry
14. he was ravenously hungry
15. she was eaten up by hunger
16. feasted as if they had been hungry for a month
17. suddenly realized that he was appallingly hungry
18. he began to be sensible that he was hungry, not having eaten for some time
19. never in my life was I so hungry
20. a hungry stomach has no ears
21. seemed to eat with a hungry appetite
22. when he is hungry there is a certain appearance of voracity about him
23. his hunger increased in course of time
24. she was so hungry that she would not wait
25. about the middle of the day she gets hungry
26. his eyes looked so awfully hungry
27. he looked terribly like a hungry old dog

WT
WAIST

WT101 WAIST 101

1. a belt around her waist defined its smallness
2. bent almost double
3. bent over to
4. bowed with much dignity
5. bowing slightly from the waist
6. executed a little bow
7. he bent double
8. he leaned anxiously forward
9. naked to the waist
10. leaned to lift
11. stooping to

WT102 WAIST 102 (SIDES)

1. sobbing with the pain of a stitch in her side
2. one hand pressed to his side
3. he turned on his side and willed himself to sleep
4. was sobbing with the pain of a stitch in her side

WT103 WAIST 103 (TOUCHING WAIST)

1. folding her hands at her waist
2. he caught her at the waist with both hands
3. he put his arms around her waist and pushed her up the stairs
4. he wrapped his arms around her midriff
5. his arms firmly around her waist
6. his arms encompassed more than her waist
7. his hands explored the soft lines of her back, her waist, her hips
8. his strong hands circled her waist and lifted her down
9. putting his arm around her waist, he squeezed her affectionately
10. putting a hand to her waist, he drew her form to him

11.   came up behind him, her arms locking around his waist

BK
BACK

BK101 BACK 101

1.   there was an angry bloody welt across her back
2.   he nodded at the man's back
3.   turned her back on him sharply
4.   turning his back on her
5.   he bowed
6.   he disappeared down the block, his back ramrod straight, his arms pumping like crazy
7.   he prowled the rug, arms behind his back
8.   he stooped
9.   her back straightened
10.   her body arched from the hips
11.   his back became ramrod straight
12.   holding his hands behind his immense back
13.   leaning his back against
14.   watched his broad back
15.   turned his back on her
16.   was slouching

BK102 BACK 102 (SPINE)

1.   pressing her spine against the door
2.   he stiffened his spine
3.   putting his hands on his hips, he bent his torso backwards until his spine cracked

BK103 BACK 103 (TOUCHING BACK)

1.   her back arched against him, her hips moving with his

2.   the concave hollow of her spine tingled at his touch
3.   thumping on the back
4.   trailed tickling fingers up and down his back
5.   wound her arms inside his jacket and around his back
6.   caressed the length of his back
7.   laid his hand gently on the bowed back
8.   his hands moved gently down the length of her back
9.   his arms encircled her, one hand in the small of her back
10.   his fingers pressing into her back
11.   he rubbed the bare skin of her back and shoulders
12.   his hands caressed the planes of her back
13.   his hands explored the hollows of her back
14.   his hands explored the soft lines of her back, her waist, her hips
15.   his hands locked against her spine
16.   his hands locked together behind his back
17.   put her hand to her aching back

BK104 BACK 104 (FEELING SENSATIONS)

1.   could feel the sudden perspiration on her back and between her breasts
2.   sent a crawling chill up his back
3.   there was a raw streak of pain across her back
4.   his backbone melted
5.   could feel the sudden perspiration on her back and between her breasts
6.   her back ached between her shoulder blades
7.   straightened to relieve the ache in her shoulders
8.   stretched his aching back
9.   stretched the ache from his back

BK105 BACK 105 (LYING ON BACK)

1.   catching her shoulders, he turned her over onto her back

2. turned on her back
3. catching her shoulders, he turned her over onto her back

BK106 BACK 106 (SUPPORTING THE BACK)

1. trying to brace herself, sitting with her back to the wall, her arms round her knees
2. consciously kept her back straight
3. closing the door, leaned her back against it
4. hands behind his back, he stiffened his massive weight

BT
BUTTOCKS

BT101 BUTTOCKS 101

1. he slapped her buttocks
2. he swatted her behind
3. his derriere high in the air
4. rocking on his backside
5. sitting on his haunches
6. squatted back on his haunches
7. with an affectionate slap on the flank
8. buttocks swung so freely and provocatively as to invite
9. it fit closely over her buttocks
10. gave a smart blow upon his buttocks
11. swaying her buttocks amorously

HP
HIPS

HP101 HIPS 101

1. her hips tapered into long straight legs
2. his hands lifted her robe above her hips

3.	his stance emphasized the force of his thighs and the slimness of his hips
4.	he swung his sword comfortably onto his hip

HP102 HIPS 102 (MOVING HIPS)

1.	tilting her shoulders one way, her hips another
2.	rolled his hips lubriciously
3.	arched her hips to meet him
4.	hooked her thumb in her panties and cocked her hip
5.	instinctively, her hips lifted in a sensuous invitation
6.	with both hands on her hips, confronted him
7.	tilting her shoulders one way, her hips another
8.	her back arched against him, her hips moving with his
9.	moved lightly but with enough hip sway to pull her skirt in opposite directions
10.	giving him a hip-cocked pose
11.	her body arched from the hips

HP103 HIPS 103 (TOUCHING HIPS)

1.	put her hands on her hips
2.	standing with one hand upon her hip
3.	threw back her head and placed her hands on her hips
4.	sitting on a bench, haunch to haunch
5.	her back arched against him, her hips moving with his
6.	a nudge here, a hip there, and an occasional light shove
7.	putting his hands on his hips, he bent his torso backwards until his spine cracked
8.	felt a jolt as his thigh brush her hip
9.	his body became taut, and he stood hovering over her, his hands on his hips
10.	his hands explored the soft lines of her waist, her hips
11.	he placed his hands belligerently on his hips
12.	he stood over her, his hands on his hips
13.	his hand explored the soft lines of her back, her waist, her hips

14.   his hand moved under her dress to skim her hips and thighs
15.   his hands resting on his hips
16.   one hand slid down her taut stomach to the swell of her hips

AR
ARMS

AR101 ARMS 101

1.   he had his arm protectively around her shoulders
2.   resting an arm protectively on the back of the chair
3.   buried her head in her arms
4.   rested her head on her arms
5.   wrenched her arm free from his grasp
6.   arm went limp
7.   arm lying across
8.   arms folded tightly
9.   he began to slip his hands up her arms, ever so slowly
10.   he placed a restraining hand on her arm
11.   he hunched over, his arms resting on his thighs
12.   he halted her escape with a firm hand on her arm
13.   he shifted his weight to his arms as if to rise
14.   he was massaging her arm in a circular motion
15.   her head up, her arms folded tight as a gate
16.   his arm firmly around her waist
17.   his arms spread expansively
18.   his hand slid down her arm and tightened around her wrist
19.   his fingers stroked her arm sensuously
20.   his fingers slid sensuously over her bare arm
21.   his pointing arm was serpentine
22.   leaned his crossed arms atop a
23.   lifting her head, straining back against his arm
24.   lugging in her arms
25.   nursing his right hand and arm against his chest
26.   opening her arms

27. planting palms flat against the surface, he exerted full strength, straining muscles on arms and shoulders
28. put her arms around
29. raising open arms
30. reaching for the solid strength of his arm
31. let it swing for a moment on her arm
32. lifted her arms to cover her breasts
33. folded her arms across her chest
34. stretched out her arms to touch him
35. placed her hand on his forearm
36. crossed her arms
37. stretching his arm across the back of her seat
38. stretching her arms over her head
39. swinging back her arm
40. the muscles of his forearm hardened beneath the sleeve
41. threw up one arm
42. with his left arm across the back of the seat, he twisted around and said
43. coiling the rope over his arm

AR102 ARMS 102 (HOLDING SOMEONE)

1. he put his arms around her and held her close
2. he turned to her without waking and held her close against him
3. he gathered her tightly against his chest
4. held him close, ignoring the stiffness in her shoulders
5. slowly, he put out his arms and drew her toward him gently
6. could feel his uneven breathing on her cheek, as he held her close
7. embraced him and kissed his cheek, her arms solid and strong around him
8. crushing her to him, he pressed his mouth to hers
9. linked arms with him and led him toward
10. felt his fingers on her elbow, then an arm was around her shoulders
11. clung to him even harder

12.   clinging to him desperately
13.   he held her so tightly could hardly breathe
14.   gently removed her arm from his protective clutch
15.   he pulled her against him gently
16.   felt an arm around her shoulders
17.   he had his arm protectively around her shoulders
18.   felt his steadying arm around her
19.   he threw a boisterous arm around her shoulder
20.   her arms encircling his neck, drawing him down toward her
21.   clinging together, as if the touch of flesh against flesh was a defense against the insanity
22.   embraced him more closely
23.   gathering her into his arms, he held her snugly
24.   gently he rocked her back and forth
25.   grasping his arm
26.   he clasped her body tightly to his
27.   he put his arms around her waist and pushed her up the stairs
28.   he slipped her hand through the crook of his arms and squeezed
29.   her to him
30.   he swung her into the circle of his arms
31.   he placed a restraining hand on her arm
32.   he pulled her roughly, almost violently, to him
33.   he swept her, weightless, into his arms
34.   her arm trapped in his iron fingers
35.   his fingers took her arm with gentle authority
36.   his embrace encompassed more than her waist
37.   his hands tightened on her arm
38.   his arms encircled her, one hand in the small of her back
39.   his flesh met hers in a warm clasp
40.   his hands slipped up her arms, bringing her closer
41.   in one forward motion, was in his arms
42.   could feel his uneven breathing on her cheek, as he held her close
43.   gripped his arms above the elbows
44.   had no desire to back out of his embrace
45.   dreamed of being crud within his embrace

46. longed for the protectiveness of his arms
47. relaxed, sinking into his cushioning embrace
48. locked herself in his embrace
49. settled back, enjoying the feel of his arms around her
50. wound her arms inside his jacket and around his back
51. struggling not against him but with him
52. suddenly was lifted into the cradle of his arms
53. taking her full weight as flew into his arms
54. the warmth of his arms was so male, so bracing
55. throwing herself into his outstretched arms

AR103 ARMS 103 (HUGGING)

1. he threw a boisterous arm around her shoulder
2. he threw his arm around her shoulders roughly
3. he put his hands on her shoulders, drawing her to him
4. felt his fingers on her elbow, then an arm was around her shoulders
5. put her arms around his neck
6. he pulled her against him
7. he gathered her tightly against his chest
8. slowly, he put out his arms and drew her toward him gently
9. trying to brace herself, sitting with her back to the wall, her arms round her knees
10. embraced him and kissed his cheek, her arms solid and strong around him
11. reclaiming lips, he crud her to him
12. hugged herself as the tears began to fall
13. raised her arms suddenly and threw them around his neck
14. clung to him even harder
15. he flung out his arms expansively at the sight of his visitor and embraced him
16. clutching her pillow to her chest
17. he felt the warmth of her flesh beneath her thin silk shirt as he folded his arms around her and pressed her against him
18. hugged herself as the tears began to fall
19. hugged her knees with a shiver

20. drew her knees up to her chin and hugged them
21. her arms wrapped around her pillow like a child holding a favorite doll
22. putting his arm around her waist, he squeezed her affectionately
23. hugged him proudly
24. embraced him and kissed his cheek, her arms solid and strong around him
25. snuggled into his embrace
26. hugged her arms to her
27. hugged her knees to her
28. put her arms around his neck
29. clutched him about
30. putting his around her shoulders
31. her arms around the pillow
32. crossed her arms, trying to ease the discomfort

AR104 ARMS 104 (RESTRAINING SOMEONE)

1. for half a second he moved to try to restrain her
2. they forced his arms behind him, tying them brutally tight with a leather thong
3. her arms pinioned helplessly at her sides by his grip
4. before could move he grabbed her, pushing her back against the cushions
5. he put a warning hand on her arm
6. clung to him, wanting the kiss to go on
7. he caught her wrist and, forcing her arm backward, held it pressed for a moment on the top of the wall
8. impulsively clutched his arm
9. clung to him even harder
10. tore herself out of his arms
11. he was holding her too hard, his fingers digging into the flesh of her arm
12. he pulled her against him gently
13. he caught her arms and spun her around
14. his arm pinioned hers as kissed her fiercely

15. clutched his arm
16. he held her easily
17. flung out an arm quickly to catch at him
18. had him in a rear hug hold
19. pulling away with a tearing reluctance
20. pulled away, fighting back the tears
21. yanked away from him
22. struggling free, her blue eyes blazing, faced him furiously
23. twisting in his arms and arching her body, sought to get free
24. without looking away, backed out of his grasp
25. threw herself at him and clung to his arm

AR105 ARMS 105 (CARRYING SOMETHING/SOMEONE)

1. her weight was exhausting him, tearing at the muscles of his arms and shoulders
2. calmly picked up a child under each arm
3. he unceremoniously picked her up
4. he gently lowered her feet to the ground
5. her weight was exhausting him, tearing at the muscles of his arms and shoulders
6. bodily he lifted her and laid her on the bed
7. he half carried her out to
8. he folded the paper under his arm
9. tucked beneath his arm
10. he half dragged, half carried her
11. he bent and, flinging his arm behind her knees, he scooped her off her feet

AR106 ARMS 106 (RAISING ARMS)

1. lifted her arms to cover her breasts
2. he moved his hand from her throat, catching her wrists instead, clamping them above her head while with his free hand he began to pull open her bathrobe
3. he brought his wrist up in front of his face and stared at his watch

4. flung her arm across her closed eyes and shivered before lying still again
5. rubbed his forearm across his face
6. he raised his hand as if to strike her, and then thought better of it
7. obediently raised her arm and held it suspended over her head
8. put her arm across her eyes
9. holding out his arms for
10. flung her arm across her closed eyes and shivered before lying still again
11. he cocked his arm
12. he threw his arms up, fists balled
13. put his arms behind his head and rested back against his hands
14. wiped her arm across her nose
15. lay back on the bed, her arm across her face
16. raised her arm in a signal

AR107 ARMS 107 (LOWERING ARMS)

1. abruptly he let his arm fall
2. his left forearm rested on his knee

AR108 ARMS 108 (MOVING ARMS)

1. waving his arms to draw their attention
2. flung out her arm with a little painful cry
3. arching his arm through the air, he gestured at their surroundings
4. gesturing broadly with his right arm
5. he gestured toward the door with a flourishing wave of his arm
6. his arms pumping like crazy
7. pectoral muscles in perfect colloquy with the movement of his arms

8.   rubbed his forearm across his face
9.   talking with wide sweeps of his arms
10.   opened up her arms to him
11.   helped guide it to lips
12.   he sat back and folded his arms
13.   shook off his hand

AR109 ARMS 109 (EMPTY)

1.   her arms felt empty, desolate

AR110 ARMS 110 (GESTURES)

1.   waving his arms to draw their attention
2.   greeted him with open arms
3.   slowly, he put out his arms and drew her toward him gently
4.   was patting his arm reassuringly
5.   with a wave of his arm he called her to him

AR111 ARMS 111 (FOLDING)

1.   crossed her arms, trying to ease the discomfort in her breasts
2.   lifted her arms to cover her breasts
3.   his arms folded across his chest
4.   folded her arms across her chest
5.   he stood, arms folded across his chest
6.   folding his arms, he waited for
7.   he folded his arms, straightening
8.   he folded his arms and leaned with interest against

AR112 ARMS 112 (EXTRACTING FROM EMBRACE)

1.   extricated herself from his arms slowly
2.   he pushed her away from him so he could see her face

3.   gently he held her away from him
4.   he pushed her away reluctantly
5.   straining back against his arm tossed her head
6.   gently moved away from him
7.   he tore his arm out of her grasp
8.   he disengaged himself gently
9.   he straightened and firmly pushed her away
10.   gently he tried to release himself from her arms

AR113 ARMS 113 (SUPPORTING SOMETHING)

1.   put her head in her arms and wept
2.   her face buried in her arms
3.   his left forearm rested on his knee, his head hung forward
4.   he put his arms behind his head and rested back against his hands
5.   rested her head on her arms

AR114 ARMS 114 (FLEXING)

1.   pectoral muscles in perfect colloquy with the movement of his arms

AR115 ARMS 115 (STRAINING)

1.   the child was heavy in her arms and could feel them beginning to ache

AR116 ARMS 116 (ARM PITS)
1.   stuck his hands under his armpits
2.   concealed under the armpit
3.   whipped the crutch out of his armpit
4.   clapped the sharp-edged dagger under her armpit
5.   portfolio tucked under his armpit
6.   a motion as mentioned of the region of the armpit
7.   grasping the armpit

8.   armpit rested on
9.   caught it under his armpit, and hung suspended
10.   his hat under his left armpit
11.   tucked his crutch under his armpit
12.   passed through the armpit
13.   he kept it under his armpit
14.   caught under the armpit
15.   an artery in the armpit

EB
ELBOW

EB101 ELBOW 101

1.   he touched her elbow, guiding her a little to the left
2.   felt his fingers on her elbow, then an arm was around her shoulders
3.   pushed her sleeves up to the elbows, unconsciously businesslike
4.   took her elbow in her hand and firmly guided her toward
5.   he turned, his elbow over the back of his seat
6.   he caught her by the elbows, pulling her hard against him
7.   her sleeve had slipped back to her elbow
8.   her elbows hung over the back of her chair
9.   he touched her elbow lightly, urging yet protective
10.   hooked one elbow over the backrest of his chair
11.   stubbornly remained at his elbow
12.   gripped his arms above the elbows
13.   was abruptly caught by the elbow and firmly escorted

EB102 ELBOW 102 (SUPPORTING BODY)

1.   he rested his elbows on his knees and put his head in his hands

2.   he put his elbow on the table and rested his chin in his hand
3.   pushing herself up onto her elbow
4.   leaning her elbow on the table, rested her chin in her hand
5.   hoisted herself up on her elbow
6.   planting an elbow on her upper knee, rested her chin on her cupped hand
7.   settled his elbows on the desk and steepled his fingers
8.   sat with her elbows spread
9.   his elbows firmly spread upon the table
10. he rolled over onto his elbows
11. he leaned forward, resting one elbow hard on the arm of her chair
12. he raised himself up on one elbow
13. he put his elbows on the table
14. he leaned sideways, his elbow on the back of his chair
15. he leaned forward, his elbows on the table

HN
HANDS

HN101 HANDS 101

1.   a change in the pressure of his hands on her shoulders
2.   a protective hand pressed her closer to him
3.   a movement of her hand
4.   as soon as her reaching fingers touched the warmth of his outreached hand, felt safe
5.   clenching and unclenching her right hand
6.   covering her hands with his own
7.   cupped her hands as if to receive
8.   fists were trembling
9.   fists were clenched
10. folding her hands in a pose of tranquillity
11. folding her hands at her waist
12. hands moved with desperate speed

13. hands folded on his belly
14. hands held out in a confession of ignorance
15. hastily drew her hand away
16. he cupped her chin tenderly in his warm hand
17. he pushed his hands deep into his pockets
18. he took hold of her hand and pulled her back
19. he reached out and caught her hand in his
20. he put his hand under her chin, turning her toward him
21. he clutched her hand with both of his
22. he stood over her, his hands on his hips
23. he wound a hand in her hair
24. he put his hand on her shoulder in a possessive gesture
25. he rubbed the back of his hand across his mouth
26. he spread his hands regretfully and shrugged
27. he halted her escape with a firm hand on her arm
28. he pulled his hand free of hers
29. he drove his fist into the palm of his hand
30. he dusted off his hands
31. he cupped the glasses in his hand
32. he held up a hand to silence her
33. held out her closed fist
34. held up her hand
35. held up her hand for silence
36. her hands moved of their own will
37. her hands were trembling
38. her slender hands unconsciously twisted together
39. her right hand was behind her
40. her hand clenched
41. her hand trembled
42. her hand fell
43. her hands, hidden from sight, twisted nervously in her lap
44. her hands tightened
45. her hand tremored
46. her lively hands spoke of
47. his hand came down over hers possessively
48. his hands rested on the desk, motionless, like empty gloves
49. his hands resting on his hips

50.   his hands trembled with eagerness
51.   his hand slid down her arm and tightened around her wrist
52.   his hand shoved in his pockets
53.   his free hand moved recklessly to her neck
54.   his strong hands circled her waist and lifted her down
55.   laid his hand gently on the bowed back
56.   lifting one hand, he slipped his fingers under the shoulder strap
57.   nursing his right hand and arm against his chest
58.   put his arms behind his head and rested back against his hands
59.   putting his hands up to push the wet hair off his face
60.   reaching for the solid strength of his arm
61.   restlessly, her hand stroked the arm of the chair
62.   returning the squeeze of her hand
63.   turned away, her hands clenched stiffly at her sides
64.   made a graceful gesture
65.   smoothed his leg with her hand
66.   flung out her hands in simple despair
67.   held out her hands
68.   smoothed his hair with her hand and loved him with her eyes
69.   made to give it back
70.   found that her hands were shaking
71.   stretched a hand to him
72.   never dreamed his hands would feel so warm, so gentle
73.   threw her hands over her face
74.   withdrew her hand quickly and turned away
75.   raised her hand to shelter her eyes
76.   felt his hand brush the hair from her neck
77.   threw up her hands
78.   pushed back a wayward strand of hair
79.   felt her fists bunching at her sides
80.   placed her hand on his forearm
81.   reached out and clutched at his hand
82.   threw up her hands in disgust
83.   couldn't keep her hands out of
84.   withdrew her hand

85.   sighing pleasurably under his hands
86.   slamming a hand on the desk in front of him
87.   slamming his hand down on
88.   slipped it hurriedly through his hands
89.   spread her hands out in a gesture implying
90.   spread her open hands to shield
91.   standing with one hand on her hip
92.   the fingers of his out-held hand curled up to form a cup
93.   the warmth of personal contact in his hand
94.   then his hands relaxed, resting lightly on her
95.   threw up her hands in frustration
96.   threw up her hands
97.   throwing up his hands, he sighed
98.   waved him to silence
99.   with both hands, he held it at breast level

HN102 HANDS 102 (RAISING HANDS)

1.   put her hands up to her eyes
2.   her hands had come up automatically
3.   raised her hands in an expansive gesture of compliance
4.   he raised her fingers to lips for one lingering kiss
5.   held their hands away from their swords in surrender
6.   throwing up his hands, he sighed
7.   he held out his hand suddenly and, taking hers, raised it to
        lips
8.   raised her hand to shelter her eyes
9.   smoothed her brow with both hands
10.   he raised his hand and lightly passed it over her face, closing
        her eyes
11.   raised her hands and pulled out the pins that held it
12.   unsteadily raised her hands to
13.   raised her arms suddenly and threw them around his neck
14.   he raised his hand gently to her temple and then almost
        guiltily let it fall
15.   tentatively raised her hand

16. he concealed a smile in his hand
17. took a few staggering steps backward, her hands held out in front of her
18. raised the cup to her mouth with a shaking hand
19. half raised her hand as though waving him aside
20. shading their eyes from the light that pierced the high branches of the Scots pines
21. he raised his hand to the knocker
22. he raised his hands in a primitive gesture of reassurance
23. threw his hands high above his head
24. raised her hands toward her face, clawing at him frantically
25. raising his hand as if he wanted to clout him

HN103 HANDS 103 (LOWERING HANDS)

1. he raised his hand and gave her a stinging slap across the face
2. put her hands firmly in her pockets
3. he raised his hand gently to her temple and the almost guiltily let it fall
4. his hands fell slowly to his sides
5. he smacked it down with a violence close to anger
6. her skirt tucked up, her hands on one knee
7. his hand fell back without touching her

HN104 HANDS 104 (MOVING HANDS)

1. his free hand moved recklessly to her neck
2. his hands went to his head
3. waving it under his nose
4. her hand shot out to steady herself
5. almost without realizing had done it, moved her hand slowly across the table to his
6. he did not actually touch, merely passed the flat of his palm over
7. he fanned the air with his hands in disgust
8. his hand moved with blurring speed
9. drew an invisible pattern on the tablecloth

10.   stretched out both hands and moved them
11.   he held out his hand to her for the glasses
12.   shoved her hands deep in to the pockets of her jeans
13.   his hands twitched involuntarily as he clenched and
       unclenched his fist

HN105 HANDS 105 (UNMOVING HANDS)

1.   her hand stopped in mid-stroke
2.   her hands rested on the smooth stone
3.   her hands clasped in front of her
4.   her hands hanging loosely over the armrests
5.   tried to raise her hand but her hands were too heavy to raise

HN106 HANDS 106 (FOLDED HANDS)

1.   her hands were loosely clasped in her lap
2.   clasped her hands around her ankles
3.   her hands were clasped before her

HN107 HANDS 107 (FOLDING SOMETHING)

1.   he folded his napkin and placed it on the table

HN108 HANDS 108 (WRINGING THE HANDS)

1.   he clasped his hands pleadingly
2.   twisting her fingers nervously together
3.   twisting her handkerchief in her lap
4.   suddenly found was clutching her hands together

HN109 HANDS 109 (TREMBLING HANDS)

1.   her hand was shaking slightly
2.   cradled her head in her trembling hands

3.   her hands were shaking uncontrollably
4.   trying to steady her shaking hands
5.   her hands were shaking suddenly and clutched them together
6.   her hand was shaking so much could scarcely dial the number
7.   with hands shaking, filled the kettle, banging it against the taps in her agitation

HN110 HANDS 110 (SLAPPING)

1.   he slapped her playfully on the shoulder
2.   gave him a stinging slap across the face
3.   he slapped her playfully on the shoulder
4.   raised her whip and thwacked him smartly across the wrist with the handle
5.   he slapped his hands together explosively
6.   he swatted her behind
7.   slapped her sleeves to get rid of the crumbs
8.   slapped his head
9.   with a thud he slapped his fist into his other hand
10.   with an affectionate slap on the flank
11.   he raised his hand and gave her a stinging slap across the face

HN111 HANDS 111 (PUSHING/PRESSING)

1.   felt his hand brush the hair from her neck
2.   pushed him away
3.   tried once again unsuccessfully to push him away
4.   pushed at him desperately
5.   pressed her hand against her heart, feeling its irregular fluttering
6.   one hand pressed to his side
7.   lifted her chin with his hand
8.   the pitiless fingers tightened around her throat as fought for breath
9.   he tossed his hair back from his brow

10. pushing tendrils of hair back from her damp forehead
11. with her hand pressed to her aching forehead
12. putting his hands up to push the wet hair off his face
13. pushed at him desperately
14. he touched her elbow, guiding her a little to the left
15. put her hands firmly in her pockets
16. with her hand pressed to her aching forehead
17. he drove his hands into the pockets of his trousers, his fists clenched
18. gently pushed him down onto the sofa
19. pushed the hair out of her eyes with both hands
20. desperately tried to push him away
21. he pushed his glasses onto the top of his head
22. he straightened and firmly pushed her away
23. he pushed her into a sitting position on the bed
24. he took her elbow in his hand and firmly guided her toward
25. he pushed his way out of the door
26. he pushed her violently over onto her back
27. he pushed her, stumbling toward
28. flung his hands from her arms
29. he took his shoulder and steered him to the chair
30. he pushed away his glasses
31. pushing aside her dish
32. pressed her hand hopefully to her stomach
33. giving him a slight nudge in the ribs
34. her hands braced stubbornly at the front of her full black skirts
35. his gentle nudge brought her back from her daydreams
36. laid out with a knife-edge hard strike
37. roughly, he thrust her away from him
38. he steered her into
39. pressed her hands against her ears, rocking backward and forward in misery as tried to block out the sound
40. spreading the paper out beside him with his free hand
41. he thrust him out of his way
42. she pushed the car door open
43. pushing her hands deep into her pockets

44.   pushed her sunglasses up into her hair

HN112 HANDS 112 (PULLING)

1.   he got a grip on the rock and pulled himself across
2.   gripping a fistful of fabric, pulled with all her might
3.   his hands were on her shoulders, gently pulling her toward him
4.   he put his hands on her shoulders, drawing her to him
5.   scooped the strap of her tote bag onto her shoulder
6.   catching her shoulders, he turned her over onto her back
7.   gently he pulled the et up over her shoulders and tucked it around her
8.   he moved his hand from her throat, catching her wrists instead, clamping them above her head while with his free hand he began to pull open her bathrobe
9.   with a quick jerk he had torn the wire from the wall
10.   he put his hand out and caught her chin, forcing her face to his
11.   he put his hand under her chin, turning her toward him
12.   he pulled her down to plant a smacking kiss on her cheek
13.   pulled off the scarf, shaking her hair free
14.   he wound a hand in her hair
15.   he put his hand out and caught her chin, forcing her face to his
16.   pulled his head against her
17.   tugged a great handful of his hair
18.   pulled her plate toward her
19.   pulled herself upright
20.   he pulled it out of her clutches
21.   gently he pulled it up over her shoulders and tucked it around her
22.   pulled her hand away from him violently
23.   he pulled her roughly over onto her face and threw himself on her again
24.   pulled away from him violently

25. his hands were on her shoulders gently pulling her toward him
26. carefully he pulled her to her feet
27. he extended his hand to pull her to her feet
28. he pulled her down to plant a smacking kiss on her cheek
29. he pulled her hand from the door latch abruptly
30. he held out his hand to help her rise
31. tried to pull it away without success
32. he pulled her along behind him
33. snatching it away
34. pulled at the knot, working at the tight leather until it came free
35. he lunged forward and caught her wrist, pulling it viciously so that fell toward him
36. her scream was cut off short as he clamped his hand across her mouth, pulling her hard against him
37. he half dragged, half carried her
38. pulling her hands away at last

HN113 HANDS 113 (OPENING SOMETHING)

1. he eased the lacy cup of her bra aside
2. his hand unbuttoned her blouse, his fingers icy, but the palm fiery hot
3. shook open the newspaper
4. screwed up her kerchief and rubbed her eyes with it

HN114 HANDS 114 (CLOSING SOMETHING)

1. closed the book resolutely
2. shivered, pulling the fur closer around her throat
3. closed the door and her mind
4. slowly slipping the book shut and letting it fall

HN115 HANDS 115 (HANDSHAKES)

1. approaching with a smile and an outstretched hand
2. he extended a hand with a relaxed smile
3. an almost overpowering handshake
4. approaching with a smile and an outstretched hand
5. could still feel the warm grip of his handshake
6. met the smile and the hand which was offered
7. terrific shakings of the hand
8. he extended a cold, hostile hand

HN116 HANDS 116 (WAVING)

1. turned and waved, her smile long-range but very visible
2. waving it under his nose
3. he raised an earthy hand
4. he waved him forward
5. raised a languid hand to greet a colleague
6. a moth-wing flutter of her hand
7. he sat on the porch and waved away flies
8. quickly waved aside his hesitation
9. turned and waved, her smile long range but very visible
10. sketching a farewell wave
11. lifting his hand in a laconic greeting

HN117 HANDS 117 (GESTURES)

1. he spread his hands regretfully and shrugged
2. he put his hand for a moment on her arm, a small gesture of comfort
3. he clinked glasses with him amiably
4. raised her hands in an expansive gesture of compliance
5. he held out both hands with a broad smile
6. held their hands away from their swords in surrender
7. he held out his hand suddenly and, taking hers, raised it to lips
8. he touched his forehead slightly in a mock salute
9. gesticulating wildly behind him
10. with a gesture he dismissed her

11. he smacked the palm of his hand with
12. he gestured to her to go in ahead of him
13. he held out his hand, angled above the floor as though he held a puppet there before him, dancing at his feet
14. he indicated the empty place beside him
15. he was gesticulating
16. his hands pressed together in supplication
17. he crossed himself fervently
18. he fingered the amulet that hung at his throat
19. crossing herself quietly
20. raised his hand placatingly
21. he waved him forward
22. shook her hands in agitation
23. half raised her hand as though waving him aside
24. pressed her hand to her stomach
25. spread her knotted hands expressively
26. raised the cup in half salute
27. beckoned the food baskets forward with an imperious wave of her hand
28. make the signs against evil
29. make the sign of the cross
30. all his gestures were wide and violent
31. fling up his hands in a halting gesture
32. gave a whirling salute and stamped his feet in a left turn
33. gestured in a sweeping motion with one arm
34. gesturing that he be seated on her left
35. he folded his hands together in a comfortable gesture
36. he gestured toward the door with a flourishing wave of his arm
37. he made a slight gesture with his right hand
38. he moved in an instinctive gesture of comfort
39. he put his hand on her shoulder in a possessive gesture
40. he waved his hand in a gesture of dismissal
41. he made a dismissing gesture
42. he held out his hands, offering an apology
43. he raised his hands in a primitive gesture of reassurance
44. he said, with a cautionary lift of his hand

45.	he stopped her with a raised hand
46.	he touched his forehead slightly in a mock salute
47.	he held up a hand to silence her
48.	he held up a quieting hand he touched her cheek in a wistful gesture
49.	in a defensive gesture, folded her arms across her chest
50.	lifting his hand in an emphatic gesture
51.	made one of his rare gestures of feeling, resting a brown hand on the other's shoulder
52.	raised his glasses in concession
53.	raised his hands in a don't shoot pose
54.	flung her hands out in despair
55.	spread her hands out in a gesture implying
56.	talking nonstop, her hands gliding through the air
57.	talking with wide sweeps of his arms
58.	the gesture contained an intimacy hadn't intended
59.	mutely her hands went to her breasts
60.	raised his hand to beckon the waitress
61.	the urge to go down on her knees and then cross herself was like a primeval hangover of some strange superstition
62.	gesturing rudely
63.	with a shiver of something like defiance made the sign of the cross

HN118 HANDS 118 (TOUCHING)

1.	his hand lightly touched her hardening nipples
2.	he rested his hand awkwardly for a moment on her shoulder
3.	felt his fingers lightly touch her shoulders
4.	he laid a tentative hand on her shoulder
5.	his hands on her shoulders sent an involuntary chill through her
6.	his hands rested casually on her shoulders, causing her flesh to tingle
7.	a hand fell on her shoulder
8.	a hand descended on his shoulder from behind
9.	a hand clutched her shoulder

10. a change in the pressure of his hands on her shoulders
11. felt his hand brush the hair from her neck
12. he put his hand protectively on her shoulder
13. one hand pressed to his side
14. his hand slid under her chin
15. held her hand to her forehead, her chin almost resting on her chest
16. he cupped her chin tenderly in his warm hand
17. he ran his hands through his hair in a detached motion
18. he stroked her hair lightly, trying to memorize the touch of it beneath his hand
19. her hands pressed desperately to her face
20. laid a gentle hand on his forehead, trying to ease his pain
21. he reached forward and touched her hand
22. clapped her hands to her ears
23. he put his hand on her belly
24. touched her arm almost reluctantly
25. he clasped his hands around his knee
26. rested her chin on her hands
27. put her hand on his knee
28. a hand fell on her shoulder
29. beating her fist into her palm
30. brushing her fingers across the dark curling hair of his chest
31. caressing him with loving fingertips
32. clasping her hands in ecstasy
33. covering her hands with his own
34. cupped his mouth with his hands and sucked in his breath
35. daintily patted
36. delivered a cuff
37. feeling the raw warmth of his skin beneath her fingertips
38. finger tips scraping on stone, nails gritting
39. fingers tiptoed up her calf to her knee
40. gave slightly under her fingers
41. guided him to a chair with a finger tip touch on his shoulder
42. hands to throat
43. he loosened his hold on
44. he reached out and caught her hand in his

45.   he was massaging her arm in a circular motion
46.   he folded his hands together in a comfortable gesture
47.   he touched her elbow lightly, urging yet protective
48.   he smoothed her hair
49.   he stroked the cheek beside him with great tender fingers
50.   he touched her cheek in a wistful gesture
51.   he traced his fingertip across her lip
52.   her hand moved of its own volition from his cheek to his jaw-line
53.   her hands were surprisingly gentle
54.   her hand slid further inward along his thigh
55.   her heart seemed to rush to the spot he touched
56.   her flesh prickled at his touch
57.   her fingers drummed distractedly on her crossed knee
58.   her fingers moved across the smooth sweat-slippery flesh of his back
59.   her hand on the side of his face
60.   her hands buried in the thickness of his hair
61.   hid her face with her hand to conceal
62.   his fingers were growing tender
63.   his hand came up to cover hers for a moment of shared warmth
64.   his hand tightened on her forearm in a grip of rough affection
65.   his hand was rough and gave her a sense of protection
66.   his touch, firm and persuasive, invited more
67.   his touch upset her balance
68.   his fingers were cool and smooth as they touched hers
69.   his fingers trailed down her temple
70.   his free hand moved recklessly to her neck
71.   his finger tenderly traced the line of her cheekbone and jaw
72.   his hand unbuttoned her blouse, his fingers icy, but the palm fiery hot
73.   his fingers stroked her arm sensuously
74.   his fingers burned into her tingling skin
75.   his fingers parted the soft curling hair to stroke her
76.   his hands rested casually on her shoulders, causing her flesh to tingle

77. his hands on her shoulders sent an involuntary chill through her
78. his fingers pressing into her back
79. his fingers touched hers and had the wildest urge to jump back
80. his touch was oddly soft and caressing
81. his touch was reassuring
82. his hand remained on her shoulder for a moment too long
83. his hands explored the hollows of her back
84. holding his hands about a foot apart, the man brought palm against palm in a sharp clap, as if applauding some triumph
85. hypnotized by his touch, tingled under his fingertips
86. laughingly fought him off
87. leaning down, slowly curled her fingers in his hair
88. left and right hand were partners
89. lifting one hand, he slipped his fingers under the shoulder strap
90. lightly taking her hand
91. lightly he fingered a loose tendril of hair on her cheek
92. mockingly coy, ran her finger along her jaw
93. one hand was tapping
94. one hand fondling the length of his body
95. outlining the tips of her breasts with his fingers
96. placing his two forefingers together, he pressed them against lips
97. ran her hand gropingly up
98. restlessly, her hand stroked the arm of the chair
99. rubbed it softly
100. rubbed her aimless wandering hands
101. rubbing the sleep out of her eyes
102. running her fingers through his hair
103. running both hands down
104. pressed her hand over her face convulsively
105. wiped her hands
106. stretched out her arms to touch him
107. smoothed her brow with both hands
108. covered her face with trembling hands

109. wiped her cheeks with the back of her hand
110. rubbed her hands together in glee
111. buried her hands in his thick hair
112. made no effort to retrieve her hand
113. trailed tickling fingers up and down his back
114. was careful not to let her fingers touch his
115. put up a hand to stroke
116. touched his cheeks, he put his hand on her shoulder in a possessive gesture
117. clapped a hand to her cheek
118. smoothed his hair with her hand and loved him with her eyes
119. sighing pleasurably under his hands
120. slapping her hard across the face
121. stroked his hair
122. stroking his chin, he regarded her carefully
123. stroking her hand upon his thigh
124. taking both his hands into her own
125. tapping her knee with the fingers of one hand
126. the magic of his mouth and fingers overrode her inhibitions
127. the butterfly of his fingers searching for her nipples
128. the stroking of his fingers sent pleasant jolts through her
129. the cool brush of his fingers on her skin
130. the caress was a command
131. the skin cold beneath her fingertips
132. the soft brushing of his fingers against her cheek
133. the muscles were hard beneath her fingertips
134. then his hands relaxed, resting lightly on her
135. threw it open
136. touched her with all the gentleness he could muster
137. touching her trembling lips with one finger
138. tried to struggle from
139. without warning a hand closed over her right shoulder
140. groped for the light switch
141. his hands covering hers for a moment
142. stood there, her hand pressed to her cheek, her eyes brimming with tears
143. felt his hands on her head, slipping off the headdress

144. rested her chin on her hands
145. his crude fumblings

HN119 HANDS 119 (MASSAGE)

1. felt her resistance weakening as he moved his hands slowly from her shoulders toward her breasts, massaging them sensuously
2. a change in the pressure of his hands on her shoulders
3. he stroked her forehead, soothing her, relaxing her in spite of her sick terror
4. was conscious of his reassuring hand gently squeezing her shoulder
5. with her hand pressed to her aching forehead
6. kneaded the stiff muscles with one hand and rolled her head in a circle
7. he chafed her hand gently
8. he ran his hand up and down the deep furrow of her spine
9. her hands sledding over the muscles of his back
10. his hands massaging the satiny planes of her stomach
11. massaged his right wrist with the fingers of his left hand
12. the gentle massage sent currents of desire through her
13. pressed her hand to her stomach

HN120 HANDS 120 (WIPING)

1. wiped the spittle from his chin
2. smeared the back of his hand across his chin
3. groped for a lace kerchief and pressed it to her streaming eyes
4. wiped his hair off his forehead
5. mopped his brow
6. he wiped the back of his hand across his forehead
7. he drew his hand impatiently across his brow
8. he dusted his hands together
9. dabbing at

10.	rubbed them fretfully with the back of her hand
11.	he wiped his forehead with the back of his hand

HN121 HANDS 121 (PATTING)

1.	clapping him on his shoulders
2.	planting palms flat against the surface, he exerted full strength, straining muscles on his arms and shoulders
3.	patting his shoulder gently
4.	patted one of the children on the head
5.	was patting his arm reassuringly
6.	he rested his hand awkwardly for a moment on her shoulder
7.	he banged the guy on the back
8.	he patted his shirt in an absent, searching gesture
9.	thumping on the back
10.	patted her stomach affectionately

HN122 HANDS 122 (CONCEALING SOMETHING)

1.	crossed her hands on her breast
2.	mutely her hands went to her breasts
3.	threw her hands over her face
4.	holding his hands behind his immense back

HN123 HANDS 123 (TOUCHING SEXUALLY)

1.	his hands crud her breasts before moving on to caress her body
2.	felt his hands closing on her breasts
3.	gently he reached out and touched her breasts
4.	his hand on her breast continued to move gently
5.	his hands roamed intimately over her breasts
6.	his palms followed the curves of her breasts
7.	his hands roamed over her breasts with lust-arousing exploration
8.	her breasts surged at the intimacy of his touch

9.   her nipples firmed instantly under his touch
10.   he fondled the small globe, its pink nipple marble hard
11.   gently his hand outlined the circle of her breast
12.   felt her resistance weakening as he moved his hands slowly from her shoulders toward her breasts, massaging them sensuously
13.   his hands on her shoulders sent an involuntary chill through her
14.   his hands rested casually on her shoulders, causing her flesh to tingle
15.   feeling her body tremble as he reached inside her blouse
16.   he wound a hand in her hair
17.   her hands automatically reached for the buttons of his shirt, slipping inside to caress his chest
18.   he leaned across and put his hand on her thigh
19.   his hand moved lightly up the inside of her forearm
20.   he moved his thumb slowly across her palm toward her wrist
21.   caressing him with the instinctive movements of a woman who knew how to please her man
22.   gently his hand outlined the circle of her breast
23.   he took her hands, encouraging them to explore
24.   he fondled one small globe, its pink nipple marble hard
25.   her nipples firmed instantly under his touch
26.   her body still craved his hands
27.   her breasts surged at the intimacy of his touch
28.   her body ached for his touch
29.   her skin tingled when he touched her
30.   her skin prickled with the heat of his touch
31.   his touch sent tingles up her arm
32.   his hand seared a path down her abdomen and onto her thigh
33.   his hands searched for pleasure points
34.   his hands roamed over her breasts with lust-arousing exploration
35.   his touch was divine ecstasy
36.   his expert touch sent her to even higher levels of ecstasy
37.   his hands made heated paths up and down her body
38.   his hand lightly touched her hardening nipples

39. his hands burned a path down her bare back
40. his hands roamed intimately over her breasts
41. his hand moved under her dress to skim her hips and thighs
42. his hand roving down the back of her thighs and up again
43. his hands covered the triangle of soft, curling hair
44. his hands moved magically over her smooth breasts
45. his hands moved magically over her smooth breasts
46. his hand on her breast continued to move gently
47. hypnotized by his touch, tingled under his fingertips
48. one hand slid down her taut stomach to the swell of her hips
49. was confused by her unexpected response to his touch
50. was conscious of where his warm flesh touched her
51. sliding his hands down her back to her buttocks
52. steadily her hand ventured lower
53. taking her hand, he guided it to himself
54. the mere touch of his hand sent a warming shiver through her
55. they were able to take the time to explore, to arouse, to give
     each other pleasure
56. gently he reached out and touched her breasts
57. his crude fumblings
58. felt his hands closing on her breasts

HN124 HANDS 124 (CARESSING)

1. his hand on her breast continued to move gently
2. his hands roamed intimately over her breasts
3. his palms followed the curves of her breasts
4. his hands roamed over her breasts with lust-arousing
    exploration
5. his hands moved magically over her smooth breasts
6. he fondled the small globe, its pink nipple marble hard
7. gently his hand outlined the circle of her breast
8. caressing her shoulders gently as he pressed her against him
9. his hand remained on her shoulder a moment too long
10. a change in the pressure of his hands on her shoulders
11. caressed the strong tendons in the back of his neck

12. he stroked her forehead, soothing her, relaxing her in spite of her sick terror
13. his hand, gently insistent, moved slowly over her forehead and down her temples
14. was conscious of his reassuring hand gently squeezing her shoulder
15. stroking his chin, he regarded her carefully
16. he caressed her cheek, smiling sadly
17. her hand moved of its own volition
18. laid a gentle hand on his forehead, trying to ease his pain
19. stroked his hair
20. nervously ran her hands through her hair
21. lightly he fingered a loose tendril of hair on her cheek
22. leaning down, slowly curled her fingers in his hair
23. her hands buried in the thickness of his hair
24. he pushed stray tendrils of hair away from her cheek
25. he smoothed her hair
26. laid a gentle hand on his forehead, trying to ease his pain
27. he laid a tentative hand on her shoulder
28. her hands automatically reaching for the buttons of his shirt, slipping inside to caress his chest
29. he stroked her hair lightly, trying to memorize the touch of it beneath his hand
30. dipped the cloth in the water, soothing his fevered trembling with gentle hands
31. caressing her shoulders gently as he pressed her against him
32. caressing him with the instinctive movements of a woman who knew how to please her man
33. he picked up a lock of her hair and caressed it gently
34. he began to slip his hands up her arms, ever so slowly
35. his hands moved gently down the length of her back
36. his hands explored the soft lines of her back, her waist, her hips
37. his hand slid across her silken belly
38. his touch was light and painfully teasing
39. his hands lightly traced a path over her skin
40. his hand caressed the skin of her thigh

41. his hands caressed the planes of her back
42. moving against him, reached down to caress him
43. never dreamed his hands would feel so warm, so gentle
44. caressed the length of his back
45. caressed the strong tendons in the back of his neck
46. slowly his hands moved downward, skimming either side of her body to her thighs
47. their hands feathered over each others bodies
48. he pushed the hair back from her face with a cool hand
49. his crude fumblings

HN125 HANDS 125 (EXPLORATORY TOUCHING)

1. groped in the blackness until located
2. his hands feeling for her breasts in the low neckline of her gown
3. his hands roamed over her breasts with lust-arousing exploration
4. gently his hand outlined the circle of her breast
5. he rested his hand awkwardly for a moment on her shoulder
6. groping in the dark with gentle fingers
7. groped on the lf for
8. sniffed hard and groped in the pocket of her jeans for a soggy tissue
9. he was feeling in his pocket
10. he reached into his pockets for the keys
11. rummaged in her bag and produced her car keys
12. he fumbled in his pouch
13. he slipped his hand into the bag and drew something out
14. determinedly groped in her back for
15. was rummaging around in a drawer
16. traced her fingers lightly over his eyes and nose
17. groped behind her in a cabinet and found
18. felt him fumbling with her long skirts
19. finger tips scraping on stone, nails gritting
20. he explored her thighs then moved up to her taut stomach

21. his hands feeling for her breasts in the low neckline of her gown
22. he gave her a quivering, tentative touch
23. her thoughts fragmented as his hands and lips continued their hungry search of her body
24. his fingers pointed into the sharp angle of the corner
25. his hands explored the soft lines of her waist, her hips
26. his hands slipped inside the neckline of her blouse
27. his hands roamed over her breasts with lust-arousing exploration
28. his hands moved with slow inevitability
29. his hands began a lust-arousing exploration of her soft flesh
30. pressed his fingers into the hollows desperately hoping for but not really expecting a reaction
31. ran his finger along
32. running his hand along
33. sweeping the floor with one hand, while the other was out before him as insurance against coming up short against another wall
34. they were able to take the time to explore, to arouse, to give each other pleasure
35. he felt in his pocket for
36. began to rummage in
37. his crude fumblings
38. thrusting his hand up her skirt

HN126 HANDS 126 (RUBBING)

1. he chafed her hands vigorously
2. held his hands out to the fire and began to rub them slowly together
3. he passed his hand over his forehead
4. rubbed his chin thoughtfully
5. smoothed her brow with both hands
6. with her hand pressed to her aching forehead
7. took the cloth from her and pressed it more firmly against her head

8. wearily, rubbed her hand across her eyes
9. he rubbed her hand gently
10. her hands pressed desperately to her face
11. he rubbed his hands ruefully
12. put her hand to her aching back
13. he rubbed his chin thoughtfully
14. he rubbed his leg, stiff from
15. as talked rubbed her hands on her arms and paced
16. he rubbed the bare skin of her back and shoulders
17. nervously rubbed her fingernails with her thumb
18. rubbed it vigorously
19. rubbed them fretfully with the back of her hand

HN127 HANDS 127 (HOLDING SOMEONE)

1. his hands were on her shoulders, gently pulling her toward him
2. he put his hands on her shoulders, drawing her to him
3. felt his fingers on her elbow, then an arm was around her shoulders
4. he held her hard in front of him
5. he put his hand out and caught her chin, forcing her face to his
6. clung to him blindly
7. ached suddenly to stand up with him and take him in her arms
8. he pressed her against him
9. he pulled her against him
10. catching her shoulders, he turned her over onto her back
11. he caught her by the elbows, pulling her hard against him
12. unconsciously clutched her hand even tighter
13. a change in the pressure of his hands on her shoulders
14. caught her by the wrist
15. cupping her chin
16. dropping a handful
17. gave slightly under her fingers

18. he caught her at the waist with both hands and swung her into the boat
19. he wrapped his arms around her midriff
20. he shook her into gasping silence
21. he slipped her hand through the crook of his arm and squeezed her to him
22. he fit his fingers together
23. he picked her up and swung her around excitedly
24. he placed a restraining hand on her arm
25. he pulled her close to his side and they walked together
26. he crud her to him
27. he cupped her chin tenderly in his warm hand
28. he wound a hand in her hair
29. he halted her escape with a firm hand on her arm
30. he clutched her hand with both of his
31. he reached out and hauled her from the chair
32. her fingers held
33. his fingers clamped over her trembling chin
34. his fingers were warm and strong as he grasped hers
35. his hands locked against her spine
36. his hands tightened on her arm
37. his fingers dug into her soft flesh
38. his hand was strong, firm, protective
39. his hands locked together behind his back
40. his fingers took her arm with gentle authority
41. his fingers biting deeply into her shoulder
42. his hands slipped up her arms, bringing her closer
43. his hand lingered a moment too long in its hold
44. his arms encircled her, one hand in the small of her back
45. his large hand took her face and held it gently
46. holding her down by force
47. hugged her legs
48. in one hand was clutching
49. putting a hand to her waist, he drew her form to him
50. returning the squeeze of her hand
51. paused, looked at his hand, then shook it
52. felt as in a hand had closed around her throat

53.　came up behind him, her arms locking around his waist
54.　closed her hand over his
55.　was halted by an iron grip on her wrist
56.　gave an irritable tug at her sleeve
57.　promptly disengaged her hands
58.　reached out and clutched at his hand
59.　was shocked at the impact of his gentle grip
60.　cradled her head in her trembling hands
61.　pulled his head against her
62.　reached out, lacing his fingers with her own
63.　the offending hands gripped her upper arms
64.　the hand, massive and strong, spun her around
65.　the touch of his hand was suddenly almost unbearable in its tenderness
66.　tried to struggle from
67.　weakly clutching here and there at
68.　with his powerful hands, he yanked her to her feet
69.　spinning her around by the shoulders
70.　his eyes narrowed as he held her facing him
71.　he put his hand out and caught her chin, forcing her face to his

HN128 HANDS 128 (RESTRAINING SOMEONE)

1.　without warning a hand closed over her right shoulder
2.　his hand remained on her shoulder a moment too long
3.　he put his hand on her shoulder in a possessive gesture
4.　caught at his shoulder in a tight and demanding grip
5.　a hand clutched her shoulder
6.　he moved his hand from her throat, catching her wrists instead, clamping them above her head while with his free hand he began to pull open her bathrobe
7.　he put his arm around her and pulled her away
8.　instantly his grip tightened
9.　relaxed at last beneath the iron grip on her wrists and felt at once a corresponding lessening of pressure from his hand
10.　transferring both her wrists to one hand

11. he caught hold of her shoulders
12. he put a warning hand on her arm
13. his eyes narrowed as he held her facing him
14. his grip on her wrist tightened and pain shot through her shoulder
15. impulsively clutched his arm
16. groped at him frantically
17. his hands were bound behind him
18. sprang forward and caught his arm
19. he laid his hand on her arm
20. his hand closed over her wrist
21. clawed frantically at his hands
22. he clamped a hand over her mouth as tried to scream
23. clung to him
24. ran to him and grabbed him by the arm
25. he was holding her too hard, his fingers digging into the flesh of her arm
26. felt his grip on her wrists tighten
27. he seized her hand
28. a hand descended on his shoulder from behind
29. as his grip tightened his attitude became more serious
30. caught at his shoulder in a tight and demanding grip
31. he dragged her back hard against him
32. he pulled reluctantly away and held her at arm's length
33. he put his hand out and caught her chin, forcing her face to his
34. his hands caught hers and held them still as struggled frantically to escape
35. tried to sit up but he pushed her gently back against the pillows
36. shook off his hand
37. her scream was cut off short as he clamped his hand across her mouth, pulling her hard against him

HN129 HANDS 129 (HOLDING SOMETHING)

1. the receiver slipped slightly in her hand as perspiration started out all over her palm
2. he picked up his empty glasses and thoughtfully held it level with his face, squinting through it sideways
3. cradled her head in her trembling hands
4. with a pencil in her hand felt real
5. clinging to the doorpost for support
6. turning it over and over with trembling hands
7. her fingers were pressing white on the goblet in her hand
8. his hands gripped her cruelly tight
9. the empty goblet dangled from his fingers
10. picked up a pen and held it in front of her with both hands
11. drummed the desk top with his pen
12. he shuffled through the papers impatiently
13. he snatched the key and flipping it over his back, caught it in his right hand and bounced it in his palm
14. pointing his pipe like a pistol
15. took the glasses from him
16. his hand tightened on the wheel

HN130 HANDS 130 (POURING/SERVING)

1. took the bottle from him and poured it into the glasses, slopping a little onto the table
2. reached for the bottle unthinkingly and refilled her empty glasses
3. tipped the contents out into her lap
4. reached for the wine bottle and poured some more into her glasses
5. he picked up the wine bottle and filled his glasses
6. he pushed the glasses across the bar
7. he helped himself to another drink
8. poured herself out an inch of gin
9. reaching for the teapot, managed to pour out two cups, using both hands on the handle
10. leaned forward to top up his wineglasses

11. holding out his cup to be refilled
12. poured half an inch into the glasses
13. as was pouring he caught her wrist, forcing her to slop the whisky until the glasses was almost full
14. tipped some more whisky into her glasses
15. he pressed a wineglasses into her hand
16. he topped up her glasses
17. pouring herself some coffee
18. he poured himself half a tumbler of whiskey

HN131 HANDS 131 (FISTS)

1. gripping a fistful of
2. clenched her fists together nervously
3. flung herself at the door, beating her fists in anguish against the thick unyielding timbers
4. set her chin on her fist
5. kissed his bunched up fingers
6. clenched her fists, aching to touch him and yet not daring to move
7. he smashed his fist against the palm of his hand
8. he clenched his fists till the nails bit into his palms
9. slammed her fist on her desk, making the pens jump up in the air
10. he clenched his fist tighter
11. clenched her fists defiantly
12. his hand had closed into a fist
13. clenched her fists in her lap
14. clenched her fists suddenly
15. his knuckles went white as he clenched his fists
16. slammed her fists down on
17. found was clenching her fists violently, suddenly overcome by fear
18. clenching her fists to stop her hands from shaking
19. his hands twitched involuntarily as he clenched and unclenched his fist
20. clenching his hands against the bottoms of his pockets

21. drove his clenched fist into his palm
22. he pounded with his fist
23. he slammed one fist against the other
24. he threw his arms up, fists balled
25. his fists struck invisibly, like the mouths of snakes
26. poking his fists into the pockets of his pants
27. clenched her hand until her nails entered her palm
28. with a thud he slapped his fist into his other hand
29. thumped on it with his fist
30. her hands were fisted in her lap

HN132 HANDS 132 (PALMS)

1. his palms followed the curves of her breasts
2. planting palms flat against the surface, he exerted full strength, straining muscles on his arms and shoulders
3. he pressed a kiss in her palm before replying
4. smoothed her brow with both hands
5. he smashed his fist against the palm of his hand
6. he clenched his fists till the nails bit into his palms
7. he scooped some water into the palm of his hand
8. the palms of her hands were sweating with fear
9. he moved his thumb slowly across her palm toward her wrist
10. beating her fist into her palm
11. bounced it in his palm
12. displayed on her palm
13. drove his clenched fist into his palm
14. flipped a palm back and forth
15. flung palm out in a florid gesture
16. he brought palm against palm in a sharp clap, as if applauding some triumph
17. he pressed a kiss in her palm
18. he was running his thumb deliciously up and down her palm
19. he did not actually touch, merely moved the flat of a palm over
20. he drove his fist into the palm of his hand
21. he cupped the glasses in his hand

22. his palms followed the curves of her breasts
23. his hand unbuttoned her blouse, his fingers icy, but the palm fiery hot
24. palm met palm in a halfhearted clap
25. planting palms flat against the surface, he exerted full strength, straining muscles on arms and shoulders
26. raising her palm to her forehead
27. flattened her palms against her dress
28. clenched her hand until her nails entered her palm
29. struck him with the flat of his hand, short, vicious, hard
30. touching an imploring palm to
31. with a thud he slapped his fist into his other hand
32. he held it in his palm for a moment

HN133 HANDS 133 (THROWING)

1. with a sob flung it down
2. marked a couple more sections on the plan, then threw down her pen
3. he hurled his goblet at the wall
4. he hurled it
5. thrust her wrists at him
6. he picked up a small stone and skimmed it across the water
7. then tossed it up in his hands, speculatively
8. threw down his riding gloves
9. he dragged the shirt out of her hand and threw it down behind him

HN134 HANDS 134 (REACHING)

1. his free hand moved recklessly to her neck
2. held his hands out to the fire and began to rub them slowly together
3. he reached into his pockets for the keys
4. he reached forward and pushed her hair gently back from her face

5.   reached forward and took his hands in hers
6.   he held out his hand suddenly and, taking hers, raised it to lips
7.   reached forward tentatively and kissed her cheek
8.   he put his hand out and caught her chin, forcing her face to his
9.   he reached out toward her
10.   he reached out a hand toward her
11.   groped in her pocket for a tissue
12.   he reached forward and touched her hand
13.   grabbed at the door jamb for support
14.   reluctantly reached out
15.   reached up for a final kiss
16.   reached to touch it with longing, wistful fingers
17.   reached for the wine bottle and poured some more into her glasses
18.   held out her hands to the flames
19.   reaching into his pocked for his wallet
20.   reached for her gown
21.   his hand held out carelessly for the wine
22.   reached for the bedcover and pulled it down
23.   reached forward tentatively and kissed her cheek
24.   half reaching out toward her with his hand
25.   went to take her daughter's hand
26.   he reached into
27.   reached slowly toward
28.   reached for
29.   took the glasses from him
30.   groped for the light switch
31.   her hands were shaking slightly as reached for
32.   he took it from her
33.   he held out his hand

HN135 HANDS 135 (WRITING/DRAWING)

1.   marked a couple more sections on the plan, then threw down her pen

2.   he began to scribble
3.   with a pencil in her hand felt real
4.   scribbling in her notebook
5.   with a felt pen working with infinite care, he began to draw

HN136 HANDS 136 (CLAPPING)

1.   clapped her hands to summon

HN137 HANDS 137 (HOLDING HANDS)

1.   took her hand for a moment and held it close
2.   reached forward and took his hands in hers
3.   he raised her hand gently to lips
4.   he took her hand and raised it almost to lips
5.   almost without knowing had done it took his hand
6.   he squeezed his hand lightly and then drew away
7.   moved forward and gripped her fingers for a moment
8.   he retained her fingers in his for a moment longer than necessary
9.   he caught her hand in his
10.   he took her hand when came in
11.   he held out his hand suddenly and, taking hers, raised it to lips
12.   he seized her hands, enfolding them in his own, holding them pressed against his chest
13.   pressed her own fingers miserably over his
14.   uncharacteristically groped for his hand, giving rather than seeking comfort
15.   he put his hand on hers as it lay on the table
16.   her hand still lay beneath his on the table
17.   the touch of his fingers sent little tingles of excitement up and down her spine
18.   her fingers closed around his and squeezed his hand

19.   he took her hand and raised it almost to lips

HN138 HANDS 138 (COLD)

1.   tried to warm her poor swollen hands by breathing on them
        and tucking them under her mantle
2.   within minutes her hands were aching with the cold

HN139 HANDS 139 (TAKING/ACCEPTING SOMETHING)

1.   reached forward and took his hands in hers
2.   deftly took the unlit cigarette away from him and tucked it
        back into the box
3.   took the letter and scanned it slowly
4.   he took her hand and raised it almost to lips
5.   he held out his hand suddenly and, taking hers, raised it to
        lips
6.   took the cloth from her and pressed it more firmly against
        her head
7.   almost without knowing had done it took his hand
8.   he at last managed to take it from her flailing hand
9.   took the refilled glasses from him
10.   he took the cup from her hastily
11.   took the glasses out of his
12.   he dragged the shirt out of her hand and threw it down
        behind him

HN140 HANDS 140 (SETTING SOMETHING DOWN)

1.   guiltily put down the
2.   he set it down with a bang
3.   flung her bag down on a chair
4.   he put the glasses down, fitting it meticulously into the wet
        ring it had left on the table
5.   he folded his napkin and placed it on the table

---

6.   he put down his goblet so abruptly it slopped on the linen cloth
7.   set it down with a bang on the table

HN141 HANDS 141 (PICKING SOMETHING UP)

1.   he pulled the two sketches toward him and studied them critically
2.   doggedly he picked up his knife and fork
3.   leaned over and picked up
4.   groped for a lace kerchief and pressed it to her streaming eyes
5.   he picked up his empty glasses and thoughtfully held it level with his face, squinting through it sideways
6.   he stooped and lifted her from the ground
7.   picked up her bag
8.   he picked up the whisky glasses
9.   picked up a sandwich and nibbled the edge of it
10.   picked up a pen and held it in front of her with both hands

HN142 HANDS 142 (GIVING/OFFERING SOMETHING)

1.   he clinked glasses with him amiably
2.   he passed the letter to her
3.   thrust it at her
4.   he extended his hand to pull her to her feet
5.   held out the phone
6.   handed it over without a word

HN143 HANDS 143 (LETTING GO/RELEASING)

1.   let go of him abruptly
2.   relaxed at last beneath the iron grip on her wrists and felt at once a corresponding lessening of pressure from his hand
3.   his grip on her wrists had slackened slightly
4.   he released her abruptly and pushed his hands into his pockets

5.   squeezed his hand lightly and then drew away
6.   he let go of him abruptly
7.   dropping it as if it had burned her
8.   tearing herself from his grasp
9.   gently removed her arm from his protective clutch
10.   the book slid from her hands to the floor
11.   he let go of her so suddenly nearly fell
12.   letting her bag fall to the floor

HN144 HANDS 144 (HITTING)

1.   clapped her hands to her head
2.   flung herself at the door, beating her fists in anguish against the thick unyielding timbers
3.   he smacked his fist against the palm of his hand
4.   he smacked the palm of his hand with
5.   he slammed the palm of his hand down on
6.   slammed her fist on her desk, making the pens jump up in the air
7.   he took a furious swing at the man's face, splitting his lip so the blood spattered across his chin
8.   he brought down the leather thong across her shoulders with every inch of strength he possessed
9.   slammed her fists down on

HN145 HANDS 145 (SQUEEZING)

1.   his hands crud her breasts before moving on to caress her body
2.   was conscious of his reassuring hand gently squeezing her shoulder
3.   one hand pressed to his side
4.   the pitiless fingers tightened around her throat as fought for breath
5.   felt as if a hand had closed around her throat
6.   her hand clutched involuntarily at the pen

7. his hands cupped her breasts before moving on to caress her body

HN146 HANDS 146 (NOT TOUCHING)

1. he leaned forward as if to touch her shoulder, but he changed his mind
2. he released her abruptly and pushed his hands into his pockets
3. clenched her fists, aching to touch him and yet not daring to move
4. he found himself fighting the urge to touch her hand

HN147 HANDS 147 (AVOIDING RESTRAINT)

1. shrank away from his touch
2. frantically tried to tear her wrists free of his imprisoning hand
3. tried once again unsuccessfully to push him away
4. pushed at him desperately
5. snatched her hand away from him
6. shaking off her hand
7. he shook off the hand

HN148 HANDS 148 (SUPPORTING SOMETHING)

1. nursing his right hand and arm against his chest
2. held her hand to her forehead, her chin almost resting on her chest
3. he put his elbow on the table and rested his chin in his hand
4. rested her chin on her hands
5. set her chin on her fist
6. planting an elbow on her upper knee, rested her chin on her cupped hand
7. leaning her elbow on the table, rested her chin in her hand

8.   her chin resting upon her hand
9.   he rested his chin on one hand
10. held his forehead
11. held her hand to her forehead, her chin almost resting on her chest
12. put her face in her hands, shaking her head from side to side
13. he put his arms behind his head and rested back against his hands

HN149 HANDS 149 (CUPPING HANDS)

1.   held it cupped against his chest
2.   planting an elbow on her upper knee, rested her chin on her cupped hand
3.   he cupped her chin tenderly in his warm hand
4.   cupping her chin, he searched her upturned face

HN150 HANDS 150 (GUIDING SOMEONE)

1.   his hands were on her shoulders, gently pulling her toward him
2.   he took his shoulder and steered him back to the chair
3.   guided him with a fingertip touch on his shoulder
4.   caught him by the shoulder on either side as supports and herders
5.   he caught her shoulders and propelled her toward the window
6.   he put his arm around her and pulled her away

HN151 HANDS 151 (SHAKING SOMEONE/SOMETHING)

1.   he took her by the shoulders and shook her
2.   shaking her by the shoulder
3.   shaking the fellow back into attention by the shoulders

4. he shook her hard so that her head snapped back and forth
5. he caught her shoulders and shook her hard
6. he shook her gently

HN152 HANDS 152 (HANDS DANGLING)

1. her hands hanging loosely between her knees

HN153 HANDS 153 (HANDS IN POCKETS)

1. stuck her hands in the seat pockets of her jeans
2. he was feeling in his pocket
3. slowly her hands unclenched in the pockets of her skirt
4. he released her abruptly and pushed his hands into his pockets

HN154 HANDS 154 (KISSING HAND)

1. he raised her hand to lips and pressed a lingering kiss upon her fingers
2. he raised her fingers to lips for one lingering kiss

HN155 HANDS 155 (CLENCHING)

1. clenched her fists together nervously

HN156 HANDS 156 (UNCLENCHING)

1. flexed her hands to get a better grip
2. slowly her hands unclenched in the pockets of her skirt

HN157 HANDS 157 (HANDS ON HIPS)

1.   put her hands on her hips

WR
WRIST

WR101 WRIST 101

1.   drove with a wrist draped limply over the steering wheel

WR102 WRIST 102 (MOVING)

1.   twisting his right wrist with the aid of his other hand
2.   her hand bent painfully at the wrist
3.   to raise his hand was like trying to raise a leaden weight attached to his wrist
4.   thrust her wrists at him
5.   he brought his wrist up in front of his face and stared at his watch
6.   frantically tried to tear her wrists free of his imprisoning hand
7.   pushed her fair hair back from her face with the back of her wrist

WR103 WRIST 103 (SENSATIONS)

1.   her hand bent painfully at the wrist
2.   his grip on her wrist tightened and pain shot through her shoulder
3.   a tingling in each of his fingers, spreading up across the back of his hand, reaching his wrist, now into his forearm
4.   relaxed at last beneath the iron grip on her wrists and felt at once a corresponding lessening of pressure from his hand

WR104 WRIST 104 (TOUCHING)

1.   he lunged forward and caught her wrist, pulling it viciously so that she fell toward him
2.   was halted by an iron grip on her wrist
3.   caught her by the wrist
4.   his hand closed over her wrist
5.   raised her whip and thwacked him smartly across the wrist with the handle
6.   he felt for the pulse in her wrist
7.   he supported his wrist with his other hand
8.   his hand slid down her arm and tightened around her wrist
9.   felt his grip on her wrists tighten
10.   fingers touching his wrist
11.   massaged his right wrist with the fingers of his left hand
12.   snatched her wrist away
13.   snatching her wrist away, she stood up
14.   he released her wrists immediately
15.   he caught her wrists, clamping them above her head
16.   his grip on her wrists had slackened slightly
17.   he caught her wrist and, forcing her arm backward, held it pressed for a moment on the
18.   he moved his thumb slowly across her palm toward her wrist

FN
FINGERS

FN101 FINGERS 101

1.   the rings on his fingers winked in the candlelight
2.   his muscles tensed suddenly under her fingertips
3.   placing long callused fingers on the table before him
4.   was careful not to let her fingers touch his
5.   whispered between her fingers

FN102 FINGERS 102 (GRASPING)

1. gripping a fistful of fabric, pulled with all her might
2. with a swift tug
3. he clutched
4. his fingers took her arm with gentle authority
5. leaning down, slowly curled her fingers in his hair
6. clutched convulsively at his shirt front
7. his fingers wrapped around the dark fabric of her sleeve
8. his fingers were warm and strong as he grasped hers
9. he grasped the top of the stone wall so tightly his nails splintered
10. thrust her fingers through his thick hair
11. shook off his fingers
12. quietly closed her fingers on the folds of her skirt, holding it clear, ready to run
13. clutched the steering wheel, her knuckles white
14. clutched his arm
15. her fingers clutching the thin sheet up around her face
16. gripped his arms above the elbows
17. he fumbled in the pocket of his jacket for a pack of cigarettes
18. drew his find to him
19. grasped his tightly rolled umbrella like a sword
20. he bent forward, grasping his legs just above the knees
21. he grasped the neck of her nightgown
22. he took it with the tips of his fingers
23. his fingers fumbled with the buttons of his sweater
24. his fingers trembled in an attitude of grasping
25. took it from his grasp
26. unbuttoning her blouse with trembling fingers
27. snatched it out of his hand
28. clutched at the door
29. he snatched the paper away from her
30. his fingers feeling for

FN103 FINGERS 103 (TOUCHING)

1.   his fingers moved forward and down until they closed over her breasts
2.   the butterfly play of his fingers searching for her nipples
3.   his fingers were cool and smooth as they touched hers
4.   as soon as her reaching fingers touched the warmth of his outreached hand, she felt safe
5.   outlining the tips of her breasts with his fingers
6.   touched the tip of her finger to
7.   fingers touching his wrist
8.   touching her trembling lips with one finger
9.   fanning his fingers wide apart, he circled her breast
10. his fingers curved under her chin
11. his fingers touched hers and she had the wildest urge to jump back
12. his fingers slid sensuously over her bare arm
13. his fingers brushed her collarbone, lingering there too long to be an accident
14. ran her forefinger over
15. running her fingers through his hair
16. touched his cheeks, the skin cold beneath her fingertips
17. leaning down, slowly curled her fingers in his hair
18. his fingers took her arm with gentle authority
19. his fingers wrapped around the dark fabric of her sleeve
20. felt his fingers lightly touch her shoulders
21. felt his fingers on her elbow, then an arm was around her shoulders
22. he fingered the amulet that hung at his throat
23. touched his jacket experimentally, as if testing the command had over her fingers
24. the magic of his mouth and fingers overrode her inhibitions
25. his fingers stroked her arm sensuously
26. kissed his fingers
27. thrust her fingers through his thick hair
28. kissed his bunched up fingers

29. placing his two forefingers together, he pressed them against lips
30. he traced his fingertip across her lip
31. felt his fingers on her elbow, then an arm was around her shoulders
32. his fingertips rested on the edge of the table
33. reached to touch it with longing, wistful fingers
34. he touched her face lightly with the tip of his finger
35. felt his fingers lightly touch her shoulders
36. he fingered the amulet that hung at his throat
37. reached out, lacing his fingers with her own
38. threading his fingers through her hair, holding her face still
39. pressed her own fingers miserably over his
40. he touched her cheek gently with his finger
41. he fingered the top buttons of his shirt, drawing them together almost defensively
42. the touch of his fingers sent little tingles of excitement up and down her spine
43. ran her finger round the inside of her glasses and sucked it pointedly
44. running the dust delightedly through his fingers

FN104 FINGERS 104 (TAPPING)

1. his fingers drummed on the phone
2. he drummed his fingers on the desk top
3. tapped him on the knee reprovingly
4. he drummed his fingers on the desk
5. tapping her knee with the fingers of one hand

FN105 FINGERS 105 (MOVING)

1. her fingers moved restlessly over the cushions
2. stuck a finger in his mouth and snapped it to make a pop like a cork out of a bottle

3. he was reading slowly, his finger tracing the figures methodically down the page
4. he flexed his fingers slowly around the stem
5. his fingers moved forward and down until they closed over her breasts
6. let her fingers play for a moment in the water
7. fiddled with the clasp of her handbag
8. twisting her fingers nervously together
9. a flick of the fingers
10. he brushed aside her trembling fingers
11. waved a finger in his face

FN106 FINGERS 106 (HOLDING)

1. fanning his fingers wide apart, he circled her breast
2. holding on to the guardrail in case he slipped and fell
3. laced her fingers around his neck
4. his fingers curved under her chin
5. thrust her fingers through his thick hair
6. reached out, lacing his fingers with her own
7. threading his fingers through her hair, holding her face still
8. he retained her fingers in his for a moment longer than necessary
9. he carried his jacket over his shoulder, his finger hooked through the loop
10. the empty goblet dangled from his goblet
11. twisting his empty glasses thoughtfully between his fingers
12. fanning his fingers wide apart, he circled her breast
13. closed his fingers around the glasses and helped guide it to lips
14. his fingers took her arm with gentle authority
15. he folded the paper under his arm
16. dangling from his fingers
17. his fingers wrapped around the dark fabric of her sleeve

18.   his fingers biting deeply into her shoulder
19.   her arm trapped in his iron fingers

FN107 FINGERS 107 (GESTURING)

1.   beckoning her after him, he strode out of the hall
2.   holding her finger to lips
3.   holding a finger to lips
4.   with a snap of his fingers, he dismissed the clerks
5.   holding her finger to lips
6.   gesturing rudely
7.   with a shiver of something like defiance made the sign of the cross
8.   jerked her thumb towards
9.   pointing a finger of admonishment
10.   raised an admonitory finger
11.   waved a finger in his face
12.   whispered between her fingers

FN108 FINGERS 108 (POKING)

1.   poked at a wet eyelid with annoyance
2.   he stabbed at it with a grimy finger
3.   he flicked it with his finger
4.   flicked an imaginary speck of dirt from
5.   tapping her knee with the fingers of one hand

FN109 FINGERS 109 (GRIPPING)

1.   he got a grip on the rock and pulled himself across
2.   unconsciously, he was clutching the sides of his seat
3.   felt her fingers lock around the receiver, her knuckles white
4.   his fingers wrapped around the dark fabric of her sleeve
5.   his fingers clamped over her trembling chin
6.   kissed his bunched up fingers

7.   his fingers dug into her soft flesh
8.   he grasped the top of the stone wall so tightly his nails splintered
9.   only the whitening of her knuckles, as her fingers clutched unconsciously together, showed the turmoil inside her
10.   he found himself clutching at the arms of his chair as if to reassure himself of its solidity
11.   her fingers were pressing white on the goblet in her hand
12.   the pitiless fingers tightened around her throat as fought for breath
13.   his fingers took her arm with gentle authority
14.   he was holding her too hard, his fingers digging into the flesh of her arm
15.   her fingers closed around his and squeezed his hand
16.   reached out, lacing his fingers with her own
17.   her grip loosened
18.   leaning forward, clasped her hands together like an eager child
19.   he clutched
20.   gripped his arms above the elbows

FN110 FINGERS 110 (KNUCKLES)

1.   felt her fingers lock around the receiver, her knuckles white
2.   knuckled the rain from his eyes
3.   stroked her cheek with the back of his knuckles
4.   rubbed her eyes with her knuckles trying desperately to clear her head
5.   only the whitening of her knuckles, as her fingers clutched unconsciously together, shoed the turmoil inside her
6.   his knuckles went white as he clenched his fists
7.   clutched the steering wheel, her knuckles white
8.   bit her knuckles for a moment
9.   caressing her cheek with the knuckle of his forehand

10.   his knuckles whitened on the phone

FN111 FINGERS 111 (FINGERNAILS)

1.   picking his teeth with the corner of his thumbnail
2.   chewing her nails
3.   idly paring his nails with a knife
4.   picking his teeth with the corner of his thumbnail
5.   he grasped the top of the stone wall so tightly his nails splintered
6.   he clenched his fists till the nails bit into his palms
7.   dug her nails into
8.   he was intent on tracing the pattern with his thumbnail
9.   pierced it with her thumbnail
10.   gnawed her thumbnail
11.   clenched her hand until her nails entered her palm
12.   beneath her nails a bloody welt opened down his cheek
13.   nervously chewing her thumbnail

FN112 FINGERS 112 (CHEWING NAILS)

1.   picking his teeth with the corner of his thumbnail
2.   biting her fingernails in terror
3.   gnawed her thumbnail
4.   biting her fingertips in terror

FN113 FINGERS 113 (THUMB)

1.   beneath her nails a bloody welt opened down his cheek
2.   her thumb firmly plugged into her mouth
3.   he was intent on tracing the pattern with his thumbnail
4.   gnawed her thumbnail
5.   he moved his thumb slowly across her palm toward her wrist
6.   nervously chewing her thumbnail
7.   tested the blade gently against his thumb

8.   he jerked his thumb at
9.   he gently put his thumb and forefinger on his eyelids

FN114 FINGERS 114 (POINTING)

1.   he waved his finger past his throat
2.   he pointed over his shoulder
3.   strained her eyes into the distance to where he pointed
4.   gestulating toward
5.   looked where his finger led her
6.   he stabbed at it with a grimy finger
7.   tracing it with her forefinger

FN115 FINGERS 115 (FIDGETING)

1.   he had taken an unused spoon between his fingers,
     twisting it restless to and fro
2.   twisting it between her fingers
3.   her fingers fluttered to her neck
4.   nervously ran her hands through her hair
5.   only the whitening of her knuckles, as her fingers
     clutched unconsciously together, showed the turmoil
     inside her

FN116 FINGERS 116 (SCRATCHING)

1.   scratching harshly at
2.   beneath her nails a bloody welt opened down his cheek
3.   found she was clawing at the

FN117 FINGERS 117 (SNAPPING)

1.   he snapped his fingers at a clerk

2. with a snap of his fingers, he dismissed the clerks
3. he clicked his fingers in front of her face

FN118 FINGERS 118 (TRACING)

1. outlining the tips of her breasts with his fingers
2. he was tracing the writing of the document
3. ran her finger down the page
4. his finger tracing the lines of writing that grew smaller and more cramped toward the bottom
5. traced her fingers lightly over his eyes and nose
6. his fingers stroked her arm sensuously
7. his finger tenderly traced the line of her cheekbone and jaw
8. ran her forefinger over
9. running her fingers through his hair
10. his fingers slid sensuously over her bare arm
11. his fingers brushed her collarbone, lingering there too long to be an accident

FN119 FINGERS 119 (RUBBING)

1. his fingers moved forward and down until they closed over her breasts
2. the butterfly play of his fingers searching for her nipples
3. nervously fingered the skirt
4. he ran his fingers rather desperately through his hair
5. knuckling the rain from his eyes
6. he gently put his thumb and forefinger on his eyelids
7. his fingers stroked her arm sensuously

FN120 FINGERS 120 (SQUEEZING)

1. his fingers moved forward and down until they closed over her breasts

2. his fingers biting deeply into her shoulder
3. the pitiless fingers tightened around her throat as fought for breath
4. his fingers flexed for a moment on the smooth oak under his hand

FN121 FINGERS 121 (HOOKING WITH FINGER)

1. he carried his jacket over his shoulder, his finger hooked through the loop
2. leaning down, slowly curled her fingers in his hair
3. lifting one hand, slipped his fingers under the shoulder strap
4. lightly he fingered a loose tendril of hair of her cheek
5. thrust her fingers through his thick hair

FN122 FINGERS 122 (FEELING SENSATIONS)

1. a teardrop stood for a moment on the pad of his forefinger
2. pricking her fingers in her haste on the brooch
3. touched his cheeks, the skin cold beneath her fingertips
4. a tingling in each of his fingers, spreading up across the back of his hand, reaching his wrist, now into his forearm
5. falling out of numbed fingers
6. felt the blood surge from her fingertips to her toes
7. her thin fingers tensed
8. her fingers ached to reach over and touch him
9. his fingers were warm and strong as he grasped hers
10. his fingers were cool and smooth as they touched hers
11. the muscles were hard beneath her fingertips

FN123 FINGERS 123 (OPENING SOMETHING)

1. slid his finger under the seal

FN124 FINGERS 124 (PRESSING)

1. gave slightly under her fingers
2. his fingers biting deeply into her shoulder
3. her arm trapped in his iron fingers
4. his fingers pressing into her back
5. his fingers took her arm with gentle authority

LG
LEGS

LG101 LEGS 101

1. he felt her legs fall willingly apart to receive him
2. he rubbed his leg, stiff from
3. felt his knee forcing her legs apart
4. between her legs she was holding
5. it grazed his leg
6. he hung his legs over
7. his knees forcing her legs apart
8. lay spread-eagled
9. legs threatened to buckle under him
10. muscles of the legs lost their spring
11. water was running down her legs making pools around her feet
12. tried his legs

LG102 LEGS 102 (LAP)

1. took his head in her lap
2. clenched her fists in her lap
3. gently pushed her from his lap

LG103 LEGS 103 (CROSSING)

1.   he crossed his ankle over his raised knee
2.   he rested his ankle casually across his knee
3.   he pulled one ankle up to rest on his knee
4.   reversed her legs
5.   her right leg was wrapped around her left in a sort of boneless abandon
6.   he leaned back and crossed one long leg over the other
7.   crossed her elegantly trousered legs
8.   seated cross-legged
9.   folded up his legs

LG104 LEGS 104 (SWINGING LEGS)

1.   swung her legs over the side of the bed and stood up
2.   dropped her legs
3.   threw his leg stiffly over the pommel
4.   his legs scissored around hers
5.   throwing one leg over the corner of the table
6.   sitting up, he swung his legs to the floor
7.   reversed her legs
8.   frantically waving legs

LG105 LEGS 105 (STRETCHING LEGS)

1.   he sat on his great chair, his legs stuck out in front of him
2.   he stretched his long legs under the table
3.   stretched his legs out in front of him slowly

LG106 LEGS 106 (TOUCHING)

1.   smoothed his leg with her hand
2.   her right leg was wrapped around her left in a sort of boneless abandon

3. his legs scissored around hers
4. one thigh lay possessively across hers
5. he leaned across and put his hand on her thigh
6. his thigh for a moment brush against hers
7. her hand slid further inward along his thigh
8. his hand moved under her dress to skim her hips and thighs
9. his hand caressed the skin of her thigh
10. was fully aware of the hardness of his thigh brushing up against hers
11. felt a jolt as his thigh brush her hip
12. felt his powerful male hardness against her thigh
13. slowly his hands moved downward, skimming either side of her body to her thighs
14. stroking her hand upon his thigh

TG
THIGHS

TG101 THIGHS 101 (THIGHS)

1. one thigh lay possessively across hers
2. he leaned across and put his hand on her thigh
3. his thigh for a moment brush against hers
4. a tremor inside her heated her thighs and groin
5. exploring her thighs and then moving up
6. he patted his thigh
7. he explored her thighs then moved up to her taut stomach
8. he hunched over, his arms resting on his thighs
9. her dress crept up onto her thighs as she moved closer to him
10. her hand slid further inward along his thigh
11. his hand moved under her dress to skim her hips and thighs
12. his hand caressed the skin of her thigh
13. his knee moved to part her thighs

14. his hand roving down the back of her thighs and up again
15. his hand seared a path down her abdomen and onto her thigh
16. felt a painful ache building between her thighs
17. was fully aware of the hardness of his thigh brushing up against hers
18. felt a jolt as his thigh brush her hip
19. felt his powerful male hardness against her thigh
20. slowly his hands moved downward, skimming either side of her body to her thighs
21. stroking her hand upon his thigh
22. the muscles of her thighs and belly flexed rhythmically
23. his knee forced her thighs apart in the dark

KN
KNEES

KN101 KNEES 101

1. it fell from her knees to the floor
2. clung to him as her knees threatened to give way
3. contrived to bend his knees
4. he let it sag on his knees
5. he crouched
6. knees drawn up
7. propped on his knees
8. putting one knee on
9. set him on her knee
10. he drew her between his knees

KN102 KNEES 102 (TREMBLING)

1. blood pounded in her brain, leapt from her heart, and made her knees tremble
2. his knees jellied

3. knees quivered
4. her knees were weakened by the quivering of her limbs
5. felt her knees weaken as his mouth descended
6. nearly collapsing into the chair as her knees buckled
7. hugged her knees with a shiver
8. blood pounded in her brain, leapt from her heart, and made her knees tremble

KN103 KNEES 103 (HOLDING KNEES)

1. trying to brace herself, sitting with her back to the wall, her arms round her knees
2. put her hand on his knee
3. drew her knees up to her chin and hugged them
4. hugged her knees with a shiver
5. he clasped his hands around his knees

KN104 KNEES 104 (KNEELING)

1. threw herself on her knees in front of him
2. threw herself down on her knees beside him
3. weary beyond endurance, sank to her knees
4. knelt at his feet
5. dropped on her knees beside him
6. submitted to her punishment on her knees
7. he dropped on one knee
8. dropped to her knees
9. he shifted his weight uncomfortably from one knee to the other
10. went down on one knee
11. got on his knees
12. sank slowly to her knees
13. the urge to go down on her knees and then cross herself was like a primeval hangover of some strange superstition

14.   knelt before the altar

KN105 KNEES 105 (TOUCHING KNEES)

1.   tapped him on the knee reprovingly
2.   his knee forced her thighs apart in the dark
3.   planting an elbow on her upper knee, rested her chin on
        her cupped hand
4.   tapping her knee with the fingers of one hand
5.   he brought it down with a violent crack across his knee
6.   he rested his ankle casually across his knees
7.   his left forearm rested on his knee, his head hung forward
8.   put his head on his knees
9.   he crossed his ankle over his raised knee
10.   he bent, and flinging his arm behind her knees, he
        scooped her off her feet
11.   he crossed one knee over the other, his whole body
        relaxed
12.   felt his knee forcing her legs apart
13.   her fingers drummed distractedly on her crossed knee
14.   his knees forcing her legs apart

CV
CALVES

CV101 CALVES 101

1.   a stab of pain in his calves
2.   with a sidelong glance at her calves
3.   squatting down on his calves
4.   felt an apprehensive twitch in the calves of his legs
5.   the water rushed about the calves of their legs
6.   he rubbed his calves
7.   calves ached with the exercise
8.   it dangled about the calves of his legs
9.   dress switched about her calves

10. boots extended halfway up his calves
11. his calves were burning
12. his muscular calves encased in
13. it hit against his calves as he walked

AK
ANKLES

AK101 ANKLES 101

1. he crossed his ankle over his raised knee
2. fetched her ankle a kick
3. he rested his ankle casually across his knee
4. shuffling ankle deep through
5. slopped about ankle-deep in water
6. waded ankle-deep through the
7. dislocated and twisted his ankle
8. a place on his ankle started itching
9. fell downstairs and sprained my ankle
10. sprained her ankle so severely that she could not leave her room
11. sank ankle deep at every step
12. snatched his ankle from under him
13. did not entirely hide the pretty foot and ankle
14. scratched his ankle with the toe nails of his other foot
15. caught her by the ankle, and tripped her
16. suffered
17. great uneasiness in the joint of her left ankle
18. behind his ankle her feet entwined
19. the bones of his leg broke at the ankle
20. in leaping out of the way he turned his ankle
21. caught her by the ankle and pulled her down
22. lifting her dress to the height of her ankle
23. exposing some inches of naked ankle
24. softly rubbing her ankle
25. he clasped his ankle in his hand

26.   ankle was caught by something, and he fell headlong
27.   she thrust out a foot and ankle
28.   he lashed one end of it about her left ankle
29.   he caught him by the foot, where the ankle turns in the socket

FE
FEET

FE101   FEET 101

1.   he could not make it to his feet; the first attempt made his head whirl
2.   he rested his feet on the coffee table
3.   feeling the dew soaking into her shoes
4.   he put his foot up on the seat
5.   he gently lowered her feet to the ground
6.   climbing numbly to her feet
7.   shouted the last word, stamping her foot
8.   he jumped to his feet
9.   pushed her feet into the slippers
10.   her foot had gone to sleep
11.   after kicking off her shoes, dabbled her feet in the icy water
12.   he sat down on the edge of a table, one foot on the carpet, the other swinging slowly back and forth
13.   he swung his feet up onto the coffee table
14.   bare feet sending up little clouds of dust
15.   feet were in agony
16.   feet kicked in the air
17.   grinding his foot
18.   her feet seemed to be drifting along on a cloud
19.   lowered her feet to the ground
20.   pulled his feet under him
21.   raised his foot
22.   was sitting on both of her feet

23. rocked on her heels
24. soles of feet were growing sore
25. stretching his feet
26. with his powerful hands, he yanked her to her feet
27. water was running down her legs making pools around her feet
28. stamped her bare foot on the carpet like a child
29. he had jumped to his feet
30. he ground out his third cigarette into the grass with his heel
31. he swung on his heel
32. shuffling his feet uncomfortably

TO
TOES

TO101 TOES 101

1. standing on tiptoe, touched lips to his
2. picked it up between her toes
3. scraped his shoe tip on the floor
4. felt the blood surge from her fingertips to her toes
5. stand on tiptoe
6. standing on tiptoe, touched lips to his
7. trod painfully on her toe
8. wriggled his toes
9. tiptoed forward
10. on impulse he tiptoed back toward
11. tiptoed to the door

MU
MUSCLES

MU101 MUSCLES 101

1.   buried her face against the corded muscles of his chest
2.   ached with exhaustion
3.   tried to ignore the strange aching in her limbs
4.   the muscles were hard beneath her fingertips

MU102 MUSCLES 102 (WORKING)

1.   renewed strength coiled in her muscles
2.   saw the tiny movement of the muscles at the corner of his jaw
3.   felt a muscle somewhere in her stomach start to tense
4.   the muscles in her stomach were clenching nervously
5.   pectoral muscles in perfect colloquy with the movement of his arms
6.   planting palms flat against the surface, he exerted full strength, straining muscles on his arms and shoulders
7.   a muscle quivered at his jaw
8.   a muscle flicked angrily at his jaw
9.   saw the tiny movement of the muscles at the corner of his jaw
10.   tried to control his stomach muscles
11.   her weight was exhausting him, tearing at the muscles of his arms and shoulders

MU103 MUSCLES 103 (LOOSENING)

1.   could feel the tension leaving her body as she relaxed deeper into the cushions
2.   took a deep breath and tried to relax
3.   he allowed himself to relax
4.   stretched his aching back
5.   stretched the ache from his back

MU104 MUSCLES 104 (TIGHTENING/FLINCHING)

1.   the shock of the cold water briefly paralyzed her
2.   the muscles of his forearm hardened beneath the sleeve
3.   the cords in his neck stood out violently
4.   jaw muscles hardened
5.   cheek muscles stood out when he clenched his jaw
6.   there was an almost feline tautness about his muscles as he flexed
7.   a muscle clenched along his jaw
8.   saw the tiny movement of the muscles at the corner of his jaw
9.   felt herself go rigid
10.   his muscles tensed suddenly under her fingertips
11.   jerking upright
12.   muscles of the legs lost their spring

MU105 MUSCLES 105 (STIFF)

1.   her weight was exhausting him, tearing at the muscles of his arms and shoulders
2.   felt herself go rigid
3.   was amazed to find how stiff had become
4.   there was an almost feline tautness about his muscles as he flexed

MU106 MUSCLES 106 (WEAK)

1.   too weak to propel herself
2.   felt limp, every muscle soft and unresponsive
3.   her weight was exhausting him, tearing at the muscles of his arms and shoulders

BO
BONES

BO101 BONES 101

1. he moved slowly, as if every bone in his body were aching with fatigue
2. felt her bones dissolve in an icy trickle of terror
3. the cold bled in and her muscles began to ache
4. the arctic bath chilled her to the marrow
5. it disturbed the very marrow in his bones
6. it shook up my bones
7. could hear my bones clack when I walked
8. the spear pierced his bones
9. they fairly laughed their bones loose
10. felt it in her bones that something was about to
11. can no longer rest my bones on
12. sent a shiver to the very marrow of her bones
13. took her weary bones off to bed
14. there was a sickening sound of crushing bones
15. his brittle temper came from aching bones
16. he was afraid to the marrow in his bones
17. he was a cowering bag of bones
18. it seemed as though their bones would burst through their skins
19. their bones ached
20. they were simply so many bags of bones in which
21. kindly hands searched for broken bones
22. he sat by the fire to warm his frozen bones
23. he got up with pain enough in his bones
24. beginning to put some flesh on his bones again
25. she smoothed rouge over her cheek-bones
26. a cloak wrapped up his aged bones
27. the flesh was twitching on his bones
28. the frost that got into his bones a bit
29. chills the very marrow of our bones
30. her bones were nearly knocked out of joint
31. the bones of his leg broke at the ankle
32. every morsel of flesh in my bones shrank when he came near

33. coquetry seasons the marrow of her bones
34. the flesh quivered on his bones
35. the chill of that room penetrated his bones
36. some of the little bones of his foot were injured
37. the fall jarred all his bones
38. woke the fever in his bones
39. it took a long while to get the cold out of their bones
40. she was getting a little rusty in the bones
41. rending the very flesh from their bones
42. could tell by his bones whether there would be a severe winter or a mild one
43. warmed his old bones like
44. strength failed his bones and he fell
45. the blow to his back made his bones ring like stones in a tin can
46. he painfully dragged his aching bones along
47. misery had worn him to the bones
48. the frost pierced through all his bones
49. fear melted the marrow in her bones
50. feeling weak in all his bones
51. the wind cut the flesh off his bones
52. hunger rattled his dry bones

BY
BODY

BY101 BODY 101

1. her body was a mass of aching bruises
2. he pulled her roughly over onto her face and threw himself on her again
3. his hands cupped her breasts before moving on to caress her body
4. every curve of her body spoke defiance
5. every fiber in her body warned her against him
6. her body was slumped in despair
7. her body vibrated with new life
8. her knees were weakened by the quivering of her limbs

9.   her body felt heavy and warm
10.   her body stiffened in shock
11.   her body arched from the hips
12.   the sweetly intoxicating musk of his body overwhelmed her
13.   the touch of lips on hers sent a shock wave through her entire body
14.   the breath knocked out of his body
15.   fiercely resisted the anguished burning of her own body

BY102 BODY 102 (BODIES TOUCHING)

1.   holding him at her nipples, slid partially under him
2.   he turned to her without waking and held her close against him
3.   snuggling against his warm, relaxed body
4.   he gathered her tightly against his chest
5.   feeling her body tremble as he reached inside her blouse
6.   felt him shudder as he drew in a sharp breath
7.   felt the movement of his breathing
8.   could feel his uneven breathing on her cheek, as he held her close
9.   reclaiming lips, he crushed her to him
10.   skin to skin, they were one
11.   leaned lightly into him, tilting her face toward his
12.   he threw himself on her, pushing her violently over onto her back
13.   he felt the warmth of her flesh beneath her thin silk shirt as he folded his arms around her and pressed her against him
14.   he felt her legs fall willingly apart to receive him
15.   lying on top of her, his tongue probed between lips
16.   her slim, warm body lay on his
17.   her body seemed to cleave to his
18.   clung to him as her knees threatened to give way
19.   for a moment they clung together

20.   her arms encircling his neck, drawing him down toward her
21.   caressing her shoulders gently as he pressed her against him
22.   fell back as his weight came down on top of her
23.   a mutual shudder ran along their length
24.   aroused now, drew herself closer to him
25.   as pressed against him could feel his impatience
26.   as though his words released her, flung herself against him
27.   at last, reluctantly they parted a few inches
28.   burying himself in her softness
29.   every curve of her body molded against his
30.   glorying in the feel of her silken flesh
31.   he moved against her, fanning the sparks of arousal into a leaping flame
32.   he clasped her body tightly to his
33.   he stood so close could feel the heat from his body
34.   her body squirmed beneath him
35.   her body opened to him
36.   her trembling limbs clung to him
37.   her body understood his rhythm
38.   her body tingled from the contact
39.   her body ached for his touch
40.   her skin prickled with the heat of his touch
41.   her body melted against his and the world was filled with him
42.   her softness moved against his caresses
43.   her soft curves molded to the contours of his lean body
44.   her body burning his flesh
45.   his hard body was atop hers
46.   his body imprisoned hers in a web of growing arousal
47.   his body moved to partially cover hers
48.   his naked body claimed her
49.   his nearness kindled feelings of fire
50.   his nearness was overwhelming
51.   his legs scissored around hers

52. his knees forcing her legs apart
53. his closeness was so male, so bracing
54. holding him at her nipples, slid partially under him
55. instinctively, her body arched toward him
56. it was flesh against flesh, man against woman
57. making love with a hungry intensity
58. passionately arched to meet him
59. patiently he brought her to the brink of climax
60. plastered himself to
61. pressing himself against her from head to foot
62. writhed beneath him, eager to touch his skin
63. couldn't miss the musky smell of him as he pressed her closer
64. gasped as he lowered his body over hers
65. was gathered against a warm pulsing body
66. matched his urgency with her own lusty, unsated needs
67. moved against him in a suggestive body caress
68. curled into the curve of his body
69. lay paralyzed beneath him
70. felt the electricity of his touch
71. was enjoying his closeness
72. molded herself against him wanting more
73. could feel the heat of his body course down the entire length of hers
74. rose to meet him in a moment of uncontrolled passion
75. welcomed him into her body
76. snuggled against him as their legs intertwined
77. felt the thundering of his heart pounding against her breasts
78. skin to skin, they were one
79. steady thrusts of possession
80. struggling not against him but with him
81. the earth fell away and went with him to that place of rapture, utterly consumed
82. the sweet throbbing of lips made her shift closer to him
83. the nearness of him gave her comfort
84. the incredible power of his surging body

85.	the sleek caress of his body
86.	the sensual heat of his naked skin the feel of his rough skin against hers exalted her
87.	the shock of him ran through her body
88.	their bodies came together with the reverence of tender love
89.	and the passion of seduction, their closeness was like a drug, lulling her to euphoria
90.	their bodies were in exquisite harmony with one another
91.	they shared an intense physical awareness of each other
92.	together they found the tempo that bound their bodies together
93.	trembling against his warm, virile nearness
94.	tucking her curves into his own contours
95.	welcoming him into her body
96.	wrapping her legs tightly around him, pulled him into her
97.	pulling her hard against him
98.	fell back as his weight came down on top of her

BY103 BODY 103 BODIES TOUCHING (CHEST TO CHEST OR BREAST)

1.	gasped as bare chest met bare chest
2.	felt her breasts crush against the hardness of his chest
3.	felt the thundering of his heart pounding against her breasts
4.	gasped as bare chest met bare chest
5.	felt her breasts crush against the hardness of his chest
6.	his naked chest melded to hers
7.	her breasts tingled against his hair-roughened chest
8.	caressing her shoulders gently as he pressed her against him
9.	could feel his heart thudding against her own

BY104 BODY 104 (SENSATIONS)

1. the incredible power of his surging body
2. the sleek caress of his body
3. the sensual heat of his naked skin the feel of his rough skin against hers exalted her
4. the shock of him ran through her body
5. their bodies came together with the reverence of tender love
6. and the passion of seduction, their closeness was like a drug, lulling her to euphoria
7. their bodies were in exquisite harmony with one another
8. every fiber in her body warned her against him
9. her body was slumped in despair
10. her body vibrated with new life
11. her knees were weakened by the quivering of her limbs
12. her body felt heavy and warm
13. her body stiffened in shock
14. the sweetly intoxicating musk of his body overwhelmed her
15. the touch of lips on hers sent a shock wave through her entire body
16. the breath knocked out of his body
17. fiercely resisted the anguished burning of her own body
18. they shared an intense physical awareness of each other

BM
BODY MOVING

BM101 BODY MOVING 101 (KNEELING)

1. threw herself down on her knees beside him
2. proudly, without lowering her head, knelt before him
3. he flung himself on his knees beside her
4. sat down gratefully on a kitchen chair

5.   he shifted his weight uncomfortably from one knee to the other
6.   weary beyond endurance, sank to her knees
7.   sank slowly to her knees
8.   got on his knees
9.   he knelt at her feet
10. kneeling in front of her
11. propped on his knees
12. went down on one knee
13. he got up to kneel before her
14. dropped on her knees beside him

BM102 BODY MOVING 102 (TURNING)

1.   turned with a quick snap of his thick shoulders
2.   suddenly he swung around
3.   he turned in his chair without comment
4.   he turned to the food that had been put down before him
5.   turned away petulantly
6.   he turned abruptly on his heel
7.   abruptly he turned away
8.   he turned away from her
9.   tilted her chin up, wiped her eyes, and turned away
10. turned away, not wanting him to see the indignant tears that threatened to come suddenly to her eyes
11. turned to follow his gaze
12. he turned back toward her
13. in anguish turned away
14. he rounded on her
15. he swung to face her
16. turning back toward her
17. turned away, not wanting him to see the indignant tears that threatened to come suddenly to her eyes
18. he rolled over onto his elbows
19. whirled around
20. turned hastily to
21. swung around to look at him

22. he turned, his elbow over the back of his seat
23. he turned away sharply, trying to hide his face
24. faced him abruptly
25. turned her back on him sharply
26. with a groan rolled onto her side
27. he turned her to face him
28. stood up and turned her back to him determinedly
29. turned to face him, her eyes alive with hope
30. he swung away from her
31. swung to face him
32. he swung on his heel
33. he suddenly rounded on her irritably
34. rounded on her
35. turning his back on her
36. turned to follow his gaze
37. rolled over so that could see
38. with a curt bow, he turned away
39. backed out
40. before even turned around, knew he was there
41. by tacit consent, they both turned and walked away
42. he stopped in mid-stride and turned
43. he backtracked
44. he turned on his heel
45. he turned, easing into a smile
46. he turned on his heel and strode to the door
47. he swerved
48. he whirled to stare at her
49. he whirled
50. he turned quickly away
51. he spun and was gone
52. he spun around
53. redoubled his steps
54. rolled as he twisted aside
55. stopped suddenly and slowly turned in a circle
56. swiveled quickly, turning her back
57. turned away without waiting for a reply
58. withdrew her hand quickly and turned away

59.   turned away, her hands clenched stiffly at her sides
60.   turned abruptly
61.   turned with a start when someone touched her arm
62.   turned away, wearied by indecision
63.   swiveled slowly, her delight growing
64.   turned away, not waiting for an answer
65.   suddenly found herself being spun around
66.   the tension was gone from her face when turned to him
67.   they both turned and walked on silently
68.   turned his back on her
69.   turned her over bodily
70.   turning to face
71.   turning blindly, stumbled
72.   veered
73.   with a deliberately casual movement, turned and faced him
74.   he turned away from her and looked out the window
75.   hastily retraced her steps
76.   he turned and left her alone
77.   he turned in his seat
78.   he turned away sharply

BM103 BODY MOVING 103 (LEANING)

1.   bending forward to get a glimpse of cleavage
2.   he leaned forward as if to touch her shoulder, but he changed his mind
3.   leaned over and picked up
4.   he leaned thoughtfully on
5.   leaning back slightly
6.   the sweet throbbing of lips made her shift closer to him
7.   he reached across to kiss her cheek
8.   leaned lightly into him, tilting her face toward his
9.   he was sitting on the floor, leaning against the sofa, his head resting on the seat cushions, his eyes closed
10.   he ducked under the low doorway

11. grabbed at the door jamb for support as the blood drained from her head
12. he pushed himself away from the wall against which he had been leaning
13. he leaned forward urgently
14. he leaned sideways, his elbow on the back of his chair
15. he leaned forward, his elbows on the table
16. he leaned toward him across the table
17. he leaned forward earnestly
18. he folded his arms and leaned with interest against
19. he leaned forward suddenly
20. he reached across to kiss her cheek
21. leaned forward and put her hand on his knee
22. closing her eyes, leaned back, letting the dappled sunlight play across her face
23. he leaned over in excitement
24. he leaned back and crossed one long leg over the other
25. he leaned across and put his hand on her thigh
26. leaned back in her chair
27. he leaned forward as if to touch her shoulder, but he changed his mind
28. he leaned back, sipping the liquid contentedly
29. he leaned back on his elbows
30. he leaned toward her, his eyes cold
31. he leaned back, sizing her up
32. leaned perilously over
33. leaning down, slowly curled her fingers in his hair
34. leaning forward in his chair
35. leaning against the door for a moment, tried to gather strength
36. leaning her elbow on the table, rested her chin in her hand
37. leaning forward and downward
38. leaned lightly into him, tilting her face toward his
39. leaned against the taut smoothness of his shoulder
40. leaned back and closed her eyes
41. leaned back in her chair, relaxing and soaking up the sun

42.   leaned lightly into him, tilting her face toward his
43.   leaned to lift
44.   drew back into the room and leaned against the wall
45.   stood leaning backwards
46.   their bodies began to sway to and fro

BM104 BODY MOVING 104 (STRETCHING)

1.   bending forward to get a glimpse of cleavage
2.   he got up and stretched the ague from his shoulders
3.   he stretched his long legs under the table
4.   the sweet throbbing of lips made her shift closer to him
5.   he reached across to kiss her cheek
6.   parting lips, raised herself to meet his kiss
7.   standing on tiptoe, touched lips to his
8.   stretched out on the grass full length, her arms flopping
        above her head
9.   he stretched ostentatiously
10.   he twisted around to
11.   he stretched his arms above his head lazily
12.   he unwound his legs
13.   stretched herself with a yawn
14.   stretching his feet
15.   stretching her arms over her head
16.   stretched catlike in the sun

BM105 BODY MOVING 105 (MOVING)

1.   slid backward across the
2.   holding him at her nipples, slid partially under him
3.   moved slowly, balancing her head carefully atop her neck
4.   was suddenly galvanized into movement
5.   moved slowly, as if every bone in his body were aching
        with fatigue
6.   when he tried to kiss her, he got a cheek and a slow move
        back

7.   moved slowly, balancing his head carefully atop his neck
8.   moved away from behind the desk
9.   as if breaking free of some spell, found could move
       suddenly
10.   found herself guiltily moving to her husband's side
11.   determination directed all her movements
12.   went to stand
13.   dodged out of reach
14.   turned and pushed her way out of the room
15.   flung herself toward the door
16.   moved cautiously and winced
17.   had changed her position slightly
18.   maneuvering her heavy body with difficulty
19.   in one forward motion, was in his arms
20.   moved up to her limit
21.   moved deliberately
22.   moved against him in a suggestive body caress
23.   moved toward him, impelled involuntarily by her own
       passion
24.   moved restlessly
25.   rocking herself gently back and forth
26.   went to stand near him
27.   let herself in through
28.   let herself out into the
29.   sprung forward to help her

BM106 BODY MOVING 106 (SQUIRMING)

1.   shuffling his feet uncomfortably
2.   was itching to run off
3.   shifted uneasily in her seat
4.   wriggled free almost at once
5.   felt herself shrinking from the cold gray of his watchful
       smile
6.   shriveled a little at his expression
7.   stirred uneasily in the chair
8.   shifted his position slightly

9.   tried to wriggle sideways
10.   shifted uncomfortably in his seat

BM107 BODY MOVING 107 (BENDING)

1.   hunched for protection against the biting wind
2.   hunched over the catalog and examined it closely
3.   meticulously stooping, his eye level with
4.   stooped and lifted her from the ground
5.   stooped into the car to find
6.   stooped and kissed the top of his head
7.   doubled up again
8.   contrived to bend his knees
9.   folded up his legs
10.   ducked
11.   bowed
12.   hunched over, his arms resting on his thighs
13.   crouched in a tight ball
14.   curled luxuriously
15.   stooped slowly to pick up

BM108 BODY MOVING 108 (FOOTSTEPS)

1.   footsteps thundering down the hall
2.   tread of approaching footsteps
3.   hastily retraced her steps
4.   on impulse he tiptoed back toward

BM109 BODY MOVING 109 (STEPPING)

1.   scuttled along the top of the slope
2.   descended the stairs two at a time
3.   slowly he began to descend
4.   took a step nearer
5.   walked back toward her
6.   stepping close to her to kiss her hand

7.   blithely step
8.   bustled around
9.   drawing a step nearer to him
10. took a stride
11. stopped in his tracks
12. picked his way
13. reluctantly approached
14. stamped out furiously
15. cautiously stepped
16. edged along
17. quickened his pace
18. feet inched forward
19. stride faltered
20. feet slid
21. made directly toward
22. marched straight ahead
23. moved back a pace
24. picking her way back and forth
25. pranced ridiculously
26. reflexively started towards
27. had to step away from his tense, hard body
28. stopped as if struck
29. withdrew from his arms and moved to the right
30. shifted indignantly from foot to foot
31. stepped out of his encircling arms
32. took an abrupt step toward him
33. moved away, her jaw tightening
34. smothering a groan, stepped back
35. step carefully
36. stepped out along
37. stepping forward a little
38. stepping into their path
39. stopped short
40. taking a deep, unsteady breath, stepped back
41. treading a wary path
42. trod painfully on her toe
43. unluckily trod on

44.　　tiptoed forward
45.　　came down a few steps

BM110 BODY MOVING 110 (WALKING)

1.　　walked with shoulders drooped, gait slow and unsteady
2.　　beckoning her after him, he strode out of the hall
3.　　he walked up to her with a grin of amusement
4.　　slowly began to walk, seeing her shadow running before her across the grass
5.　　strolled slowly, blankly watching his boots crunch into the snow
6.　　slowly retraced his steps down the length of the hall
7.　　linked arms with him and led him toward
8.　　swaggered across the room
9.　　forcing her steps one by one
10.　　slowly, with shaking steps, made her way to
11.　　went to her favorite stance by the window
12.　　fell into step beside her in silence
13.　　moved awkwardly to
14.　　crossed the room in two strides
15.　　moved hastily across the room
16.　　began to walk briskly, threading his way purposefully toward
17.　　summoning every shred of dignity to her aid, walked toward him
18.　　swung out of the room
19.　　walked almost reluctantly toward them
20.　　followed him outside
21.　　hobbled painfully over the stones
22.　　flounced indignantly ahead of
23.　　hobbled stiffly away
24.　　strode past her to the door
25.　　a quick stroll
26.　　amble over
27.　　ambling along

28. bare feet sending up little clouds of dust
29. began pacing with measured dignity
30. blundered off
31. carried himself neatly erect
32. each stride was fluid
33. forced his legs to move
34. he trudged
35. looked at her intently, then strode to the door
36. disappeared quickly into the crowd
37. shambled
38. went to join
39. shuffled
40. strolled forward and extended a hand
41. trod
42. walked soft-footed
43. strode
44. walked nervously
45. entered
46. checked his long stride to match her own
47. sauntered at an easy pace
48. walked forward, stopping in front of her
49. walked briskly away
50. flowed like an amoebae
51. walked sadly
52. wandered over
53. took it straight to
54. walked up to her with a grin of amusement
55. padded
56. walk had a sunny cheerfulness
57. steps slowed as pondered
58. feet seemed to be drifting along on a cloud
59. feet dragged
60. hobbled awkwardly
61. looking up as approached, he quite openly studied her
62. marched straight ahead
63. mosey along
64. moved measuredly toward

65. moving as noiselessly as a cat
66. padding lightly
67. reluctantly, he walked, his movements stiff and awkward
68. sallied forth
69. brush past
70. moved easily but impatiently
71. hurried, not stopping to explain
72. passed through
73. strolled about, nodding at a few people as he moved
74. walked toward him across the floor
75. walked with stiff dignity
76. moved without haste, but with unhurried purpose
77. walked grandly to
78. began to weave in and out
79. the tedious process of laying one foot down after the other
80. tramped on
81. tread of approaching footsteps
82. walked with the silence of forest hunters
83. walking slowly, her hips swaying
84. wandered here and there
85. wandered hazily went across to
86. went on slowly afoot
87. with a springy bounce, was gone with long, purposeful strides
88. began to walk toward
89. strode toward
90. stood up slowly and walked across to her
91. slowly began to walk, seeing her shadow running before her across the grass
92. began to walk swiftly down the way they had come
93. went to stand in his favorite position by the window
94. sidled up to

BM111 BODY MOVING 111 (WALKING TIPTOE)

1.   tiptoed to the door

BM112 BODY MOVING 112 (WALKING SLOWLY)

1.   slowly, with a leaden heart, he walked up the passage

BM113 BODY MOVING 113 (WALKING PURPOSEFULLY)

1.   began to retrace his steps
2.   already he was striding toward the door
3.   strode grimly to the phone

BM114 BODY MOVING 114 (BACKING AWAY)

1.   dodged back toward the bedroom
2.   backed away hastily
3.   pulled the door open and stepped back abruptly
4.   moved back slightly
5.   when he tried to kiss her, he got a cheek and a slow move back
6.   without looking away, backed out of his grasp
7.   backed away from him until felt the rough stones of the wall against her back
8.   edged away from him
9.   obviously reluctant to leave, backed slowly toward
10.   backed away hastily as he took a step toward her
11.   was like a trapped animal, her shoulder pressed against the wall
12.   stepped abruptly backward
13.   took a few staggering steps backward, her hands held out in front of her
14.   gently drew away from her
15.   moved away from him slightly
16.   was backing away from him toward the phone

17.   backed away from him uncertainly
18.   took a step back in astonishment
19.   when he tried to kiss her, he got a cheek and a slow move back
20.   drew away slightly
21.   backed away from him
22.   edged away from him
23.   scrambled across the bed away from him and stood up
24.   the stepped to let her pass
25.   dodging behind her out of his reach

BM115 BODY MOVING 115 (PACING)

1.   he stood up and began pacing up and down the carpet
2.   began pacing slowly, her bare feet kicking the gown into a rhythmic billowing pattern
3.   he strode back and forth the floor excitedly
4.   he paced the room for the remaining time
5.   he worked off his excess energy by pacing

BM116 BODY MOVING 116 (RUNNING)

1.   set off at a run
2.   almost had to run to keep up with her
3.   hurled herself at the door
4.   fled through the door, her leather shoes pattering down the stairs
5.   broke into a brisk trot
6.   scuttled about impatiently
7.   trotted
8.   dodged away from him
9.   scuttled out
10.   took to his heels
11.   trotted
12.   skidded to a stop

13.   hurled herself recklessly
14.   lengthened his stride to a lope
15.   make a dash
16.   pace quickened to a lope
17.   run like a rabbit
18.   running lightly
19.   sprinting deerlike
20.   suddenly darted
21.   swiftly covered
22.   winning his way up
23.   threw herself at him and clung to his arm
24.   fled down the hall

BM117 BODY MOVING 117 (CRAWLING)

1.   slid backward across the
2.   scrabbling on the floor
3.   tried to crawl away, dragging herself across
4.   crawled
5.   crept forward
6.   inched forward
7.   snaked along
8.   wormed his way

BM118 BODY MOVING 118 (RISING)

1.   got up and stretched the ague from his shoulders
2.   rising to his feet, he pushed back his chair with sudden violence
3.   scrambled stiffly to her feet
4.   stood up anxiously
5.   pulled herself shakily to her feet
6.   leapt to his feet
7.   jumped to her feet at the sight of him
8.   rose to her feet with some difficulty
9.   stood up so abruptly had to force herself to remain still and not flinch backward

10.   swung her legs over the side of the bed and stood up
11.   pulled herself up off the sofa
12.   stood up shakily
13.   leapt to his feet
14.   scrambled to his feet
15.   it brought her upright with a jerk
16.   slowly, he climbed to his feet
17.   with a long, exhausted sigh, he stood up
18.   parting lips raised herself to meet his kiss
19.   awoke with a start and jolted upright
20.   pulled herself to her feet
21.   was on his feet first
22.   stood up and strolled out to the hall
23.   rose to his feet unsteadily
24.   stood up restlessly
25.   sitting up, he swung his legs to the floor
26.   stiffly stood up
27.   pushed herself up from the chair
28.   pulled herself upright
29.   climbed to her feet
30.   stood up hastily
31.   launched himself from the bed
32.   reluctantly he stood up
33.   ached suddenly to stand up with him and take him in her arms
34.   jumped up restlessly
35.   climbing numbly to her feet
36.   slowly he stood once more
37.   pushed herself up on the sofa, clutching at its back
38.   scrambled to his feet
39.   pulled himself painfully to his feet
40.   forced herself to climb out of bed
41.   struggled to her feet
42.   stood up in agitation
43.   stood up abruptly
44.   slowly pulled herself into a sitting position
45.   sat up, her head swimming

46. picked herself up wearily from the dust
47. tried to sit up
48. heaved herself to her feet
49. threw herself out of bed and ran to the bathroom
50. slowly he eased himself off her and sat up
51. arises abruptly
52. brought him to his feet
53. clumsily scrabbled to his feet
54. got to his feet
55. got stiffly to his feet
56. got to his feet eagerly
57. hauled himself to his feet
58. got to his feet
59. was on his feet
60. began to get to his feet
61. leaped to his feet
62. rose in one fluid motion
63. reached out and hauled her from the chair
64. scrambled to his feet
65. sank to his haunches
66. jumped to his feet
67. clambered to his feet
68. jumping up from
69. raising the upper half of his body into a seated position
70. regained his feet
71. rising to her feet
72. rocked him to his feet
73. was on her feet
74. rose fluidly from the chair
75. watched him as he rose to his feet
76. rose from her seat as if propelled by an explosive force
77. exclaimed in irritation as jumped to her feet
78. slowly uncurled herself
79. sprang to his feet
80. only dragging herself upright at last
81. got up to kneel before her
82. stood up briskly

83.   heaving herself out of her chair
84.   slowly forced herself to sit up
85.   hurled herself out of bed
86.   stood up slowly and walked across to her
87.   levered himself off the sofa
88.   hoisted herself up on her elbow
89.   saw tried to sit up but he pushed her gently back against the pillows
90.   climbed to his feet

BM119 BODY MOVING 119 (CLIMBING)

1.   got a grip on the rock and pulled himself across
2.   panting after her climb up the stairs
3.   climbed up into the bed, keeping her gown wrapped tightly around her
4.   climbed the worn staircase carefully
5.   forced herself as fast as could up the steep
6.   walked heavily up the stairs
7.   began to climb down
8.   held to
9.   winning his way up
10.   came up the stairs two at a time
11.   made as if to scramble up the bank

BM120 BODY MOVING 120 (DANCING)

1.   a balletic movement
2.   a slow rumba
3.   moved into a dance
4.   their bodies began to sway to and fro

BM121 BODY MOVING 121 (KICKING)

1. feet kicked in the air
2. fetched her ankle a kick
3. kicking his heels
4. kicked it into
5. stamped his foot upon

BM122 BODY MOVING 122 (JUMPING)

1. jumped violently
2. jumped visibly
3. bounced airily off
4. pounced
5. sprang to his feet
6. lunged
7. leaped
8. fingers touched hers and had the wildest urge to jump back
9. hurled himself
10. jumping up and down like a maniac
11. jumping up from
12. leaped backwards
13. lurching with surprise
14. ready to spring
15. springing to his feet
16. suddenly sprung up
17. stamped her bare foot on the carpet like a child
18. had jumped to his feet

BM123 BODY MOVING 123 (SKIPPING)

1. skipped with light gingerly steps

BM124 BODY MOVING 124 (SWIMMING)

1. too weak to propel herself
2. attempted a one-arm sidestroke

3. treading water
4. burst through the surface
5. kicked for the surface
6. sank into the water
7. straining against her body's natural buoyancy

BM125 BODY MOVING 125 (FIGHTING)

1. moved his hand from her throat, catching wrists instead, clamping them above head while with his free hand he began to pull open her bathrobe
2. launched herself at him
3. picked it up and held it up menacingly
4. grip on her wrist tightened and pain shot through her shoulder
5. caught her wrist and, forcing her arm backward, held it pressed for a moment on the top of the wall
6. pushed at him desperately
7. clawed frantically at his hands
8. clamped one hand over her mouth as tried to scream, as the other groped for her throat
9. pushed her violently over onto her back
10. threw her down and stood for a moment over her
11. lunged forward and caught her arm
12. tore herself out of he pushed her, stumbling toward
13. wrenched himself away
14. caught her arms and spun her around
15. almost shook the old woman in her impatience
16. felt a blinding blow across her face
17. threw herself at him and clung to his arm
18. gave her a stinging slap
19. the impact threw her against the wall
20. hands caught hers and held them still as struggled frantically to escape
21. lunged forward and caught her wrist, pulling it viciously so that fell toward him

22.   struggled frantically, feeling the pressure on her windpipe slowly increase

BM126 BODY MOVING 126 (SHIVERING)

1. gasping for breath and shivering violently
2. hands on her shoulders sent an involuntary chill through her
3. seldom stopped shivering
4. there was a quick shiver of apprehension
5. shivered unhappily
6. shuddered, then gave a taut laugh
7. shivered, pulling the fur closer around her throat
8. felt him shudder as he drew in a sharp breath
9. tongue sent shivers of desire racing through her
10. frowned with a sudden shiver of apprehension
11. flung her arm across her closed eyes and shivered before lying still again
12. shivered a little in spite of the warm furs around her shoulders
13. shuddered with disgust
14. a cold shiver spread over her as remembered
15. a delicious shudder heated her body
16. a delightful shiver of wanting ran through her
17. a shudder passed through her
18. a starburst of ecstasy, starting deep inside
19. a brief shiver rippled through her
20. a spurt of hungry desire spiraled through her
21. a thrill shivered through her senses
22. a mutual shudder ran along their length
23. abandoning herself to the spiraling climax
24. an electric shock had scorched through her body
25. an electrifying shudder reverberated through her
26. shudders began to rack him
27. as he roused her passion, his own grew stronger
28. catching fire from his flame

29. electricity seemed to arc through her
30. exploding in a downpour of fiery sensations
31. exultant sensation wafted through her in heated waves
32. fire-bolts of desire arced through her
33. gave a little shiver
34. gusts of desire shook her
35. shivered with expectancy
36. freed in her a bursting of sensations
37. shivered involuntarily
38. sensed the awakening flames within her
39. heat rippled under her skin as recognized the flush of
     sexual desire hadn't felt for months
40. impatience grew to explosive proportions
41. body ached with the promise of fulfillment
42. her body began to vibrate with liquid fire
43. whole being flooded with desire
44. virgin body was boiling at a feverish pitch
45. raw sensuousness carried her to greater heights
46. hands on her shoulders sent an involuntary chill through
     her
47. look was so galvanizing it sent a tremor through her
48. sharp shoulder blades shaking with harsh, tearing sobs he
     could not control
49. tongue sent shivers of desire racing through her
50. hunger rose and flared in her like a savage animal
51. jerked under the touch
52. love flowed in her like warm honey
53. passion inched through her veins
54. patiently he brought her to the brink of climax
55. realizing a shiver of panic
56. reflexively started sending shivers of delight through her
57. shaking in a state of absolute
58. felt a shudder of humiliation
59. was hurtled beyond the point of return
60. shuddered
61. shuddered inwardly at the thought
62. gave a little shiver

63.	shattered into a million glowing stars
64.	savored the feeling of satisfaction he left with her
65.	abandoned herself to the whirl of sensation
66.	felt passion rising in her like the hottest fire, clouding her brain
67.	felt the hysteria of delight rising inside her
68.	wanted to yield to the burning sweetness that seemed captive within her
69.	was drawn to a height of passion had never known before
70.	was dismayed at the magnitude of her own desire
71.	shook with impotent rage and fear
72.	felt an awakened response deep within her
73.	was roused to the peak of desire
74.	began to shake at the fearful images built in her mind
75.	knew that the moment of ecstasy had passed
76.	yielded to the searing need which had been building for months
77.	felt a familiar shiver of awareness
78.	shivered in recollection
79.	shivered with chill and fatigue
80.	shivered under her touch
81.	shivering desperately
82.	shivers of delight followed his touch
83.	shivers of delight followed his touch
84.	shrank back sighs of satisfaction shook through his body
85.	soared to an awesome, shuddering ecstasy
86.	soaring higher until the peak of delight was reached
87.	the dormant sexuality of her body had been awakened
88.	the concave hollow of her spine tingled at his touch
89.	the gentle massage sent currents of desire through her
90.	the involuntary tremors of arousal began
91.	the real world spun and careened on its axis
92.	the pleasure was pure and explosive
93.	the mere touch of his hand sent a warming shiver through her
94.	the moment of ecstasy exploding all around her

95. the tremor of released tensions
96. the hot tide of passion raged through both of them
97. the turbulence of his passion swirled around her
98. the final explosion of physical sensation
99. the fires of expectation were out of control
100. the flames of passion burned within
101. burned within both of them
102. the passion of his ardor mounted
103. the eager tremors of ecstasy
104. trembling with fury
105. trembling from the world of wondrous sensations
106. trembling against his warm, virile nearness
107. visibly trembling with intensity
108. waves of ecstasy throbbed through her
109. had begun to shiver violently
110. shuddered visibly
111. shivered violently, curling up for moment as tightly as could to try to find some warmth
112. wrapped her coat around her tightly, trying to stem the sudden, agonized shuddering that racked her body
113. was shivering violently
114. gave a shiver
115. found was shivering violently once more
116. shuddered violently
117. shivering in spite of herself
118. felt the warning prickle under her skin
119. felt a tremor of warning
120. half closed her eyes with a shiver
121. had begun to shake violently
122. felt a shiver touch her shoulders
123. gave a little shiver
124. realized, with a shock, that was shaking from head to foot
125. felt a shiver of unease stir deep down inside her
126. felt a shiver run across her shoulders
127. jumped guiltily
128. hugged her knees with a shiver

129. looking at her with eyes that made her shiver with desire
130. gave a little shudder of longing
131. felt a sudden shiver of fear
132. shuddered theatrically
133. with a shiver pulled her cloak around her
134. leaving her shaking like a leaf
135. had begun to shiver violently
136. shuddered visibly
137. could feel herself shaking with anger
138. felt a sudden shiver
139. shivered violently in spite of the warmth
140. with a shudder stood still
141. frowned with a sudden shiver of apprehension
142. felt the skin on the back of her neck prickle
143. with a shiver of something like defiance made the sign of the cross
144. stood shivering, feeling the warmth of the evening sun sinking through her shirt and into her bones
145. felt a quick shiver of warning touch his skin
146. flung her arm across her closed eyes and shivered before lying still again

BM127 BODY MOVING 127 (TREMBLING)

1. it left her shaking like a leaf
2. was shaking, half with fatigue and fear, half with anger
3. felt herself beginning to tremble
4. chin trembled
5. drew a deep breath and forbade herself to tremble
6. was trembling so violently could hardly stand
7. was shaking violently

BM128 BODY MOVING 128 (ROCKING)

1. wept aloud, rocking back and forth

2. swayed gently
3. pressed her hands against her ears, rocking backward and forward in misery as tried to block out the sound

BM129 BODY MOVING 129 (BOWING)

1. bowed without comment, his face carefully neutral, and withdrew
2. bowed slightly
3. dropped to one knee
4. gave a mocking bow
5. bowed amiably enough
6. gave her a mock bow
7. bowing slightly toward her
8. with a curt bow, he turned away

BM130 BODY MOVING 130 (CURTSYING)

1. curtsied to the ground
2. curtsying one last time as reached the door, as protocol demanded
3. curtsying to the ground
4. curtsied formally
5. dropped him a haughty curtsy
6. swept a deep curtsey
7. curtseyed low
8. bobbed a small curtsey

BM131 BODY MOVING 131 (STRAIGHTENING)

1. straightened to relieve the ache in her shoulders
2. pulled himself together with difficulty
3. suddenly he squared his shoulders
4. straightening his shoulders

5. made a visible effort to pull herself together
6. raising her chin, assumed all the dignity could muster
7. straightened, sighing loudly
8. grinned and straightened his shoulders
9. straightened abruptly
10. pushed himself away from the wall against which he had been leaning
11. straightened and firmly pushed her away
12. folded his arms, straightening
13. slowly straightened up
14. drew herself up
15. held herself upright, holding in her stomach
16. straightened defiantly

BM132 BODY MOVING 132 (ADVANCING)

1. took a protesting step forward
2. stepped menacingly toward him
3. took a step toward him
4. pushed past her
5. forcing herself to follow steadily
6. stepping close to her to kiss her hand
7. rose from the shadows and came toward her
8. with every ounce of courage possessed, stepped forward to greet him
9. preceded her around the
10. staggered very slightly as he moved toward her
11. had moved after her with extraordinary and silent speed
12. sprang forward and caught his arm
13. took a step toward her
14. summoning every shred of dignity to her aid, walked toward him
15. lunged forward
16. moved purposefully toward her
17. moved with sudden speed toward her
18. walked almost reluctantly toward them

19.	lunged toward her
20.	was immediately behind her
21.	moved toward her with astounding swiftness
22.	came toward her suddenly
23.	walked back toward her

BM133 BODY MOVING 133 (APPROACHING SOMEONE)

1.	threading her way toward them
2.	pushed his way past him into the room
3.	walked up to her with a grin of amusement

BM134 BODY MOVING 134 (LEAVING)

1.	marching away smartly, head high, chest out
2.	already he was striding toward the door
3.	let herself out of the apartment
4.	bowed without comment, his face carefully neutral, and withdrew
5.	turned abruptly on his heel
6.	abruptly, retreated indoors
7.	groped for the door, then flung himself out
8.	without another word, he strode away
9.	looked heavenward and disappeared back into the hall
10.	beckoning her after him, he strode out of the hall
11.	flung out of the room
12.	let herself out the door
13.	turned back toward the gate
14.	stood up and strolled out to the hall
15.	crept out of the room and closed the door silently
16.	without looking to see if followed, he left
17.	disappeared into her sitting room
18.	went out without a backward glance and ran out of sight
19.	watched him stride toward the doorway, expecting him to turn, but he didn't

20. walked away miserably
21. pushed out of the door
22. e made his way out of
23. tore herself away from him
24. threaded her way swiftly out without a backward glance

BM135 BODY MOVING 135 (AVOIDING RESTRAINT)

1. pulled away somewhat haughtily from his grasp
2. tore herself out of his hands
3. flung herself at the door, beating her fists in anguish against the thick unyielding timbers
4. desperately tried to turn away, but he caught her chin, forcing her to look at him
5. shrank away from his touch
6. tried once again unsuccessfully to push him away
7. tore herself away with a choking cry
8. edged away from him
9. gently moved away from him
10. ducked past him, and dodged his grasp

BM136 BODY MOVING 136 (RESTRAINING SOMEONE)

1. they forced his arms behind him, tying them brutally tight with a leather thong
2. her arms pinioned helplessly at her sides by his grip
3. before could move he grabbed her, pushing her back against the cushions

BM137 BODY MOVING 137 (CURLING)

1. shivered violently, curling up for a moment as tightly as could to try to find some warmth

BM138 BODY MOVING 138 (FOLLOWING)

1. forcing herself to follow steadily
2. with her close behind him he raced toward
3. was walking a couple of paces behind her

BM139 BODY MOVING 139 (THE PROCESS OF SITTING UP)

1. sat up, her head swimming

BM140 BODY MOVING 140 (TRYING TO RISE)

1. fighting to make her heavy limbs move, climbed out of bed
2. without conscious thought tried to get up
3. pushing away the heavy clogging sleep, struggled to sit up
4. took deep breaths until was strong enough to raise her head
5. aroused herself from the numbness that weighed her down
6. struggled to sit up
7. tried to raise her head, then, with a groan, let it fall back on the pillows

BM141 BODY MOVING 141 (READJUSTING POSITION)

1. holding him at her nipples, slid partially under him
2. tried to slump in her seat
3. slumped deeper in the passenger seat
4. slumped back onto the bed
5. subsided onto the chair
6. turned in his chair without comment
7. made a visible effort to pull herself together
8. pushing herself up onto her elbow
9. tilted her chin up, wiped her eyes, and turned away

10.   grinned and straightened his shoulders
11.   hunched over the catalog and examined it closely

BM142 BODY MOVING 142 (MARCHING)

1.   marching away smartly, head high, chest out

BM143 BODY MOVING 143 (SUPPORTING BODY)

1.   braced himself against the seat
2.   trying to brace herself, sitting with her back to the wall, her arms round her knees

BS
BODY STOPPING

BS101 BODY STOPPING 101 (UNABLE TO MOVE)

1.   was galvanized into action
2.   for a moment was too shocked to move
3.   her bruised body refused for a moment to respond as tried to ease her position
4.   her feet felt heavy, as if they no longer belonged to her
5.   tried to move her feet, but somehow they would not obey her
6.   tried to sit up, but a black silken web seemed to be holding her down
7.   tried to raise her hand but her hands were too heavy to raise

BS102 BODY STOPPING 102 (STOPPING)

1.   was brought up short
2.   stopped dead as the door swung back against the wall

3.   paused as he was about to put on his jacket
4.   stopped in his tracks
5.   brought up against an unseen wall with force enough to drive breath out of his body in a gasping grunt
6.   stopped in her tracks
7.   came to an abrupt stop
8.   stopped short in dismay
9.   they both froze in a stunned tableau
10.   stopped dead in the doorway

BS103 BODY STOPPING 103 (NONE)

1.   was paralyzed by that sense of futility that sometimes overcame even the best of men
2.   as a dead weight, resistant to her every effort, he was virtually immovable
3.   for a moment he could not move
4.   stood up so abruptly had to force herself to remain still and not flinch backward
5.   did not dare move
6.   stared at her for a moment, incapable of moving
7.   for a moment he didn't move
8.   stopped struggling as his grip on her wrist tightened and pain shot through her shoulder
9.   head bowed and remained in an attitude of frozen stillness
10.   resolutely sat still
11.   paused, reluctant to move
12.   had not moved
13.   fought desperately to remain still
14.   hovered for a moment
15.   felt herself go rigid
16.   wanted to fight him but could not move and could not speak
17.   with a shudder stood still
18.   did not follow him

19.   made herself go limp

BS104 BODY STOPPING 104 (STIFFENING)

1.   slowed the car with a jolt of fear
2.   jerked backward in his hands
3.   felt herself tense nervously
4.   started guiltily
5.   body went rigid
6.   trying to brace herself, sitting with her back to the wall, her arms round her knees
7.   tensed suddenly, realizing he was standing beside her
8.   stiffened and haughtily tossed her head
9.   jumped violently
10.   froze
11.   flinched at the double-edged cut to his meaning
12.   felt herself go rigid
13.   went completely rigid, but did not struggle
14.   with a shudder stood still
15.   drew herself up

BS105 BODY STOPPING 105 (HIDING)

1.   buried her head in his shoulder
2.   buried her head in her arms

BS106 BODY STOPPING 106 (COWERING)

1.   felt herself shrinking from the cold gray of his watchful smile
2.   shrank back
3.   flinched visibly beneath her scorn
4.   crouched lower, cowering away

BS107 BODY STOPPING 107 (SLUMPING)

1.   slumped deeper in the passenger seat

2.   sagged toward him
3.   slumped back onto the bed
4.   sat slumped in her chair
5.   shoulders slumped with despair

BS108 BODY STOPPING 108 (LYING DOWN)

1.   flopped onto the bed with a grateful sigh
2.   stretched out on the grass full length, her arms flopping above her head
3.   flung himself on the bed, staring up at the ceiling
4.   lay back on the bed, her arm across her face
5.   climbed into bed and lay back tensely
6.   went to lie face down

BS109 BODY STOPPING 109 (THE PROCESS OF SITTING DOWN)

1.   sat down abruptly next to her
2.   hitched herself up on the edge of the desk
3.   threw herself down on the sofa
4.   sat down comfortably next to her
5.   threw himself on the sofa
6.   perched on a stool
7.   perched himself uncomfortably in the corner
8.   went to sit obediently at his side
9.   sat down on the edge of the bed
10.   pulled out the chair opposite her and eased herself into it
11.   threw herself back into her chair
12.   sat bolt upright suddenly
13.   sitting down close to her
14.   sat down resolutely
15.   pushed her into a sitting position on the bed
16.   sat down heavily opposite her
17.   gingerly lowered herself onto the sofa
18.   slid into a chair
19.   slipped into the chair opposite him

20. hauled himself wearily onto a stool
21. sat back in the chair and settled his shoulders against the cushions
22. perched himself on the edge of the coffee table
23. hitching herself up onto the desk
24. flung herself down in the armchair
25. sank thankfully into her chair
26. sat down on the edge of a table, one foot on the carpet, the other swinging slowly back and forth
27. threw himself down opposite him
28. flinging himself down in a chair
29. sat down feebly, wrecked
30. settled hipshot against the corner of the desk
31. sat back, stung
32. sat down, damp and dumpy and radiating bleakness
33. squeezed herself into the driver's seat
34. slumped dejectedly into the couch and curled her feet under her
35. squatted back on his haunches
36. crouched beside
37. climbed in beside her
38. with an effort sat upright again
39. threw himself into a chair
40. sat down opposite her
41. threw himself down on the sofa
42. seated himself unobtrusively in a corner of the room
43. sat down abruptly on one of the folding chairs

BS110 BODY STOPPING 110 (FALLING)

1. was knocked off his feet
2. sagged toward him
3. fell heavily, his legs buckling under him
4. missed his footing on the stairs
5. threw herself to the far side of the bed
6. had fallen first to her knees, then slowly down until was sprawled on the grass

7. clung to him as her knees threatened to give way
8. fell back as his weight came down on top of her
9. a headlong stumble
10. careened
11. collapsed like a rag doll
12. constantly tripping
13. dropped down
14. fell heavily full length
15. fell head foremost
16. flinging herself prone across
17. flopping down upon
18. flopped down
19. stumbled away
20. pitched down
21. collapsed
22. it was sinking anguish which caused her to stumble
23. legs threatened to buckle under him
24. let himself roll across
25. nearly collapsing into the chair as her knees buckled
26. plumped down
27. sank to the floor
28. sent him sprawling to the ground
29. flopped onto the bed with a grateful sigh
30. fell into a chair
31. fell forward
32. staggered back
33. stumbled determinedly
34. swaying very slightly
35. threw herself down
36. tossed himself back
37. trying to keep his footing
38. tumbling head over heels
39. tumbling clumsily
40. flung herself back on the pillows
41. the impact of it threw her against the wall
42. throwing herself into her outstretched arms

BS111 BODY STOPPING 111 (STAGGER/STUMBLE)

1. flailed forward
2. staggered out weakly
3. staggered a couple of paces back
4. her boots slipped on the wet, muddy grass
5. could not make it to his feet; the first attempt made his head whirl
6. staggered very slightly as he moved toward her
7. preened herself visibly
8. was hampered by her heavy skirts
9. staggered a few steps away from her

BIR
BODY IN REPOSE

BIR101 BODY IN REPOSE 101 (LYING ALONE)

1. flung her arm across her closed eyes and shivered before lying still again
2. slept like a baby, on his back
3. flung her arm across her closed eyes and shivered before lying still again
4. lay half on his side
5. lay sprawling
6. flopped down
7. laid up for rest
8. lay spread-eagled
9. let himself roll across
10. lowered himself down
11. lying prone on the
12. plumped down
13. sprawled at ease
14. tossed himself back
15. turned on her belly
16. turned on her back
17. turning on her stomach

18. was lying on her side
19. lay back, huddled beneath the covers, trying to get warm

BIR102 BODY IN REPOSE 102 (LYING WITH SOMEONE)

1. turned to her without waking and held her close against him
2. assumed the superior position
3. her trembling limbs clung to him
4. gently he eased her down onto the bed
5. relaxed, sinking into his cushioning embrace
6. he lay spread-eagled over her numbed body, his head between her breasts
7. tried to dislodge the dead weight that pinned her to the bed
8. for a long time he lay unmoving, feeling the woman's body limp beneath his

BIR103 BODY IN REPOSE 103 (ALREADY SEATED POSITIONS)

1. subsided onto the chair
2. sat slumped in her chair
3. sat on his great chair, his legs stuck out in front of him
4. was seated on the edge of her chair
5. trying to brace herself, sitting with her back to the wall, her arms round her knees
6. sat very still, his eyes narrow
7. threw herself back into the chair wearily
8. jerked upright in his chair
9. went to his chair and lowered himself into it
10. throwing one leg over the corner of the table
11. pushed his chair back slightly and shifted in it sideways, draping his arm across its back, totally relaxed
12. sat preening himself

13. shifted uncomfortably in her seat
14. sat forward suddenly
15. leaned forward suddenly
16. sat forward with interest
17. sat forward on the edge of her seat
18. balanced the chair on its two back legs, lolling in it comfortably
19. pushed herself forward in the chair
20. put his foot up on the seat and clasped hands around his knee
21. sitting in the place of honor
22. shifted uneasily in her seat
23. sat unmoving, listening to the echoing silence
24. leaned back in her chair
25. shifted uncomfortably in his seat
26. curled up in the chair as if withdrawing from the fear
27. flopping down upon
28. for a long moment they sat in perfect rapport
29. did not realize how bone-aching tired he was until he sat down
30. dropped down beside her facing her
31. sat waiting
32. sat down in a huff
33. sat as if on thorns
34. sat relaxed
35. sat forward and looked at her intently
36. sat on the porch and waved away flies
37. sat propped against a tree, panting from exertion
38. sat, right foot on left knee
39. sat very still, his eyes narrow
40. slammed his swivel chair level
41. stretched his long legs casually before him
42. flopped down
43. wedged himself into the seat next to her
44. settled himself
45. hooked one elbow over the backrest of his chair
46. plonked down

47.   plumped down
48.   pulled his feet under him
49.   raising the upper half of his body into a seated position
50.   sat humped up
51.   sat back into the seat
52.   sat with sneakers angled on the floor like frogs' feet
53.   sat with the ramrod posture of a British brigadier
54.   seated cross-legged
55.   drew her legs up, placing her feet on the chair seat
56.   fell into a chair
57.   rocked back gracefully on her heels
58.   sat hunched on the edge of the king-sized bed
59.   settled into the deep cushions
60.   stirred uneasily in the chair
61.   leaned back in her chair, relaxing and soaking up the sun
62.   slid gracefully into the chair
63.   huddled in her chair
64.   jolted upright
65.   sat without moving
66.   had a chance to sit back
67.   sat back, momentarily rebuffed
68.   sat in lonely silence
69.   sat in practiced repose, hands in lap, ankles crossed
70.   rocked
71.   was sitting on both of her feet
72.   sank down
73.   shifted fretfully in his seat
74.   sitting half turned away
75.   sitting on a bench
76.   haunch to haunch
77.   sitting on his haunches
78.   sitting there, coat opened, knees wide, he took up an awful lot of room
79.   slung himself down
80.   sprawled at ease
81.   stiffly sat in a straight-backed chair

82.   the warm bulk of the woman sitting next to him urged his thighs nearer to the window
83.   they sat silently for a long time
84.   tossed himself back
85.   tucked one leg under her
86.   was sitting leaning
87.   with his left arm across the back of the seat, he twisted around and said
88.   leaned back
89.   rocked back on his seat
90.   was lying back in her chair passively
91.   was sitting on the floor, leaning against the sofa, his head resting on the seat cushions

BIR104 BODY IN REPOSE 104 (STANDING)

1.   standing, straightened her shoulders and cleared her throat
2.   stand with shoulders up
3.   was standing before him completely submissive
4.   stood up shakily
5.   went to her favorite stance by the window
6.   he threw her down and stood for a moment over her
7.   stood rigid
8.   stood submissively before him
9.   was standing by the door, her hand on the latch
10.   stood by the door holding it open as he walked past
11.   stood haughtily by as
12.   stood, one foot on a stool
13.   balancing smoothly
14.   effectively blocking
15.   feet were firmly planted
16.   he stood back a trifle sullenly
17.   he stood resolutely
18.   he stood rigid
19.   he stood over her, his hands on his hips
20.   he paused rather nervously

21.   he took his place
22.   he stood up, smiling with satisfaction
23.   he stood easily
24.   he stood there, boldly intimidating
25.   he stood so close could feel the heat from his body
26.   her bearing was stiff and proud
27.   pushed herself to a standing position
28.   stood motionless in the middle of the room
29.   straightened herself with dignity   stood and watched,
      silently waiting to see
30.   stood there, blank, amazed, and very shaken
31.   jerked to her feet
32.   stiffened at the challenge
33.   stood on tiptoe
34.   stood aside
35.   stood frozen in the doorway
36.   stood slumped over
37.   snatching her wrist away, stood up
38.   stand on tiptoe
39.   standing shoulder to shoulder
40.   standing, straightened her shoulder and cleared her throat
41.   standing sheep-like
42.   standing erect
43.   standing with one hand upon her hip
44.   stood for a long moment
45.   stood exposed
46.   stood leaning backwards
47.   stood wobbling on one leg
48.   stood dabbling her feet
49.   stood hesitating
50.   stood terribly still
51.   stood with his back to
52.   there was no time to stand and stare
53.   with his powerful hands, he yanked her to her feet
54.   standing naked in front of the mirror
55.   went to stand near him
56.   stood in the doorway

57.	stood quite still, staring up at his face
58.	stood there, her hand pressed to her cheek, her eyes brimming with tears
59.	went to stand in his favorite position by the window
60.	stood unnaturally still

BIR105 BODY IN MOTION 105 (SQUATTING)

1.	crouched beside her
2.	reluctantly he squatted down beside him
3.	squatting on her heels
4.	squatted completely relaxed, his long limbs folded with the motionless ease of someone accustomed to the role of watcher

DAILY ACTIVITIES

DAP
USING A PHONE

DAP101 USING A PHONE 101 (INITIATING A CALL)

1.	had to dial three times before got through
2.	went straight to the phone and called
3.	picked up the phone and rattled the button
4.	picked up the receiver

DAP102 USING A PHONE 102 (PHONE RINGING)

| 1. | it rang for several seconds before it was picked up |
| 2. | the sudden ringing of the phone made her jump |

DAP103 USING A PHONE 103 (ANSWERING PHONE)

| 1. | the phone was answered after just one ring |
| 2. | leaned forward and picked up the receiver |

3.　　stretched across and lifted the receiver
4.　　when the phone rang stared at it for a moment before picking it up

DAP104 USING A PHONE 104 (LISTENING TO CALLER)

1.　　for a moment he listened, puzzled
2.　　came back on the line in seconds
3.　　there was complete silence on the other end of the line
4.　　heard the grin at the other end of the phone
5.　　his voice rang so clearly in the room it sounded as if he were there with her
6.　　there was an amused chuckle down the phone

DAP105 USING A PHONE 105 (HOLDING PHONE)

1.　　found she was pressing the receiver closer and closer against her ear
2.　　the receiver slipped slightly in her hand as perspiration started out all over her palm
3.　　pulling the phone onto her knee
4.　　tucked the receiver closer to his ear
5.　　could feel the receiver slipping as held it to her ear
6.　　cradled the receiver against his left ear

DAP106 USING A PHONE 106 (TERMINATING A CALL)

1.　　slammed down the phone
2.　　when he spoke the line went dead
3.　　the connection went dead
4.　　broke the connection
5.　　slammed down the phone
6.　　hung up without giving him the chance to reply
7.　　slammed the phone down at last
8.　　put the receiver down with a sigh
9.　　slammed down the phone and dialed his number
10.　　blandly he hung up

11. slammed down the receiver
12. after putting down the receiver, stared at it blankly
13. replaced the receiver
14. put down the receiver with almost delicate care
15. stared at the receiver for a moment in disbelief, then slammed it down
16. the line went dead

DAC
IN A CAR

DAC103 IN A CAR 103 (DRIVING A CAR)

1. slouched against the door as he drove
2. turning the wheel where the car wanted to go
3. was leaning forward, hunched slightly over the steering wheel
4. negotiated a tight bend in the narrow road
5. put the car into first and crawled up the hill
6. began to ease the car forward slowly
7. peered through the windshield wipers
8. rested her forehead on the rim of the steering wheel for a moment
9. clutched the steering wheel, her knuckles white
10. exhausted by the long drive through the heavy traffic
11. hand tightened on the wheel
12. engaged the gear
13. was peering through the windshield, her hand on the dash
14. the sun beat down through the windshield onto her face

DAC104 IN A CAR 104 (ACCELERATING)

1. stamped his foot down on the accelerator
2. put his foot on the accelerator and swooped past the car

DAC105 IN A CAR 105 (STOPPING)

1.   the car shuddered to a halt
2.   slowed the car with a jolt of fear
3.   pulled the car onto the grass shoulder
4.   the car screamed to a standstill
5.   slammed on the brakes again
6.   the car drifted to a halt

DAC106 IN A CAR 106 (ENTERING TRAFFIC)

1.   pulled out into the traffic with on a perfunctory glance in
        his mirror

DAC107 IN A CAR 107 (DRIVING IN REVERSE)

1.   turned in his seat and reversed up the empty road

DAC108 IN A CAR 108I (LOOKING IN REARVIEW MIRROR)

1.   glanced in the rearview mirror and waved a truck past

DAC109 IN A CAR 109 (CHANGING DIRECTION)

1.   swung the car up the lane
2.   pulled the car into the side road and drove slowly down it

DAC110 IN A CAR 110 (SLOWING DOWN)

1.   eased his foot down on the brake pedal
2.   gently applied the brakes, cutting their speed slightly

DAC111 IN A CAR 111 (PARKING)

1.   expertly slotted the car into spot

DAC112 IN A CAR 112 (GETTING OUT OF CAR)

1.	swung the car door open and pulled herself out
2.	pushed the car door open
3.	climbed out of the car

DAD
DRESSING

DAD101 DRESSING 101 (PUTTING ON CLOTHES)

1.	dragged on her jeans
2.	paused as he was about to put on his jacket
3.	holding out his arms for the new tunic
4.	pulled on her bathrobe
5.	pushed her feet into the slippers
6.	held out her arms for her thick fur-lined cloak
7.	easing her aching limbs into the shift
8.	reached for her bathrobe from the back of the door and folded it around her
9.	knotting the belt
10.	pulling the knot of her belt tighter
11.	tucking his shirt into the waistband of his trousers
12.	tightened the belt of the bathrobe
13.	drew herself up, holding in her stomach as her gown was laced up

DAD102 DRESSING 102 (WEARING CLOTHES)

1.	eyes traveled to her breasts, outlined beneath the low-buttoned blouse
2.	taut nipples strained against the thin fabric
3.	nipples, taut beneath the thin fabric
4.	breast tingled against the fabric
5.	bed-gown had fallen open to reveal her full breasts, half swathed in her long copper hair
6.	the rich outlines of his shoulders strained against the fabric
7.	massive shoulders filled the coat he wore

8.   draped it grandly about his naked shoulders
9.   covered her shoulders
10.   shirt was damp from the heat
11.   drove his hands into the pockets of his trousers, his fists clenched
12.   with a little automatic gesture twitched her skirt straight
13.   pushed her sleeves up to the elbows, unconsciously businesslike
14.   carried his jacked over his shoulder, his finger hooked through the loop
15.   wrapped her coat around her tightly, trying to stem the sudden, agonized shuddering that racked her body
16.   opened the buttons of her shirt and turned back the collar
17.   bed-gown had fallen open to reveal her full breasts, half swathed in her copper hair
18.   tunic unlaced at the throat
19.   pulled her sash more tightly around her waist
20.   sleeve had slipped back to her elbow
21.   wearing only her bra and briefs
22.   was wearing jeans and a deep red silk shirt, unbuttoned at the throat
23.   her breasts, outlined beneath the low-buttoned blouse, seemed more prominent than usual
24.   pushing her hands deep into her pockets
25.   was wearing white jeans, rolled up above the knees
26.   the long sleeves and high neck of her blouse covered the worst of her bruises

DAD103 DRESSING 103 (TAKING OFF CLOTHES)

1.   tore her shirt open and dropped his head to nuzzle her breasts
2.   started to shrug the heavy garment off his shoulders
3.   moved his hand from her throat, catching her wrists instead, clamping them above her head while with his free hand he began to pull open her bathrobe
4.   slowly he began to unbutton his shirt

5.   divested herself of her lightweight coat
6.   tore her shirt open and dropped his head to nuzzle her breasts
7.   stripped off his shirt
8.   tore off his tie
9.   kicked off her sandals
10. started to shrug the heavy garment off his shoulders
11. began to unbuckle his belt
12. hands automatically reached for the buttons of his shirt
13. wearily slipped out of her jeans
14. pulled off the blouse
15. untied her apron with her free hand
16. pulled off his raincoat, shaking it before hanging it up
17. was fumbling with the sash of her bathrobe
18. slipped off her clothes
19. after kicking off her shoes, dabbled her feet in the icy water
20. drew off her gloves
21. unclasped the brooch that held his cloak and flung the garment to the floor
22. stripped to the waist
23. hooking his forefinger into the knot of his tie and pulling it loose
24. discarding her clothes, stood naked beneath his gaze
25. slid the gown off her shoulders, down her arms
26. stripped off her clothes with speed but control
27. eased the lacy cup of her bra aside
28. undressed her slowly, worshipfully
29. hand unbuttoned her blouse, his fingers icy, but the palm fiery hot
30. hands lifted her robe above her hips
31. fingers fumbled with the buttons of his sweater
32. didn't protest when his hands sought the buttons of her blouse
33. unbuttoning her blouse with trembling fingers
34. slipped down the ribbon straps, letting the thin cotton slip to the floor

35.	unfastened her jeweled girdle and let it fall to the floor
36.	took off her shirt and then her bra	slipped off her jeans
37.	slowly unbuttoning his shirt
38.	pulled off the boot with a grunt and threw it to the floor
39.	threw off the rest of his clothes
40.	moved his hand from her throat, catching her wrists instead, clamping them above her head while with his free hand he began to pull open her bathrobe

DAD104 DRESSING 104 (CARRYING/WEARING A PURSE)

1.	easing the heavy bag on her shoulder
2.	hitching her bag up higher onto her shoulder
3.	dropped her handbag on a chair

DAD105 DRESSING 105 (LOOKING IN A MIRROR)

1.	surveyed herself critically in the polished metal hand mirror
2.	looking in something like wonder in the mirror

DAD106 DRESSING 106 (PUTTING ON MAKEUP)

1.	just enough lipstick to show that her mouth was perfect
2.	powdered her nose

DAD107 DRESSING 107 (APPLYING LOTION)

1.	he lathered on sunscreen

DARW
READING/WRITING

DARW101 READING/WRITING 101 (WEARING GLASSES)

1.	gave her a long shrewd glance over her glasses
2.	took off her glasses

3. gave her a long shrew glance over her glasses
4. glanced over her glasses at him
5. pushed his glasses onto the top of his head
6. tried to clean the steam off his glasses
7. pulled off her dark glasses, throwing them on the bed

DARW102 READING/WRITING 102 (READING)

1. was tracing the writing of the document
2. closed the book resolutely
3. ran her finger down the page
4. scrutinized the label on the wine bottle
5. finger tracing the lines of writing that grew smaller and more cramped toward the bottom
6. scanned the closely written lines
7. took the letter and scanned it slowly
8. hunched over the catalog and examined it closely

DARW103 READING/WRITING 103 (WRITING/DRAWING)

1. marked a couple more sections on the plan, then threw down her pen
2. reached for a pen and scribbled the number down

DABS
BATHING/SHOWERING

DABS101 BATHING/SHOWERING 101 (BATHING/SHOWERING)

1. stood under the cold shower until was shaking but wide awake
2. sliding down in the water until was submerged to her chin
3. soaked her hair until it turned to a jet curtain of wet silk on her back

4. stepped under the shower attachment, letting the water stream over her face and breasts
5. bent and scooped some water into the palm of his hand and splashed it over his throat
6. took another bucket of water full in the face
7. the water was still running down her legs making pools around her feet
8. rinsed her fingers under the tap
9. shaking the water from his eyes

DADWL
DOORS/WINDOWS/LIGHTS

DADWL101 DOORS/WINDOWS/LIGHTS 101 (TURNING LIGHTS ON/OFF)

1. reached to turn off the lamp
2. tugging on the light cord
3. snapping on the light
4. groped for the light switch
5. turned on the light and the darkness shrank back into the corners

DADWL102 DOORS/WINDOWS/LIGHTS 102 (OPENING DOORS)

1. pushed it open with a flourish
2. stopped dead as the door swung back against the wall
3. pulled the door open and stepped back abruptly
4. dragged the door wider
5. groped for the door, then flung himself out
6. grabbed the key and with a shaking hand inserted it in the lock
7. rattled the handle
8. raced toward the door and flung it open
9. dragged open the door
10. on impulse he opened the door

11. cautiously opened the door and peered through the crack
12. opened the door for her and ushered her out
13. threw open the door
14. flung herself toward the front door and dragged it as far open as it would go
15. pulled the door open and stood by it
16. pulled it open, irritated at t he interruption
17. stood with her hand on the handle for a moment, then, taking a deep breath, opened it
18. wrenched the doors open
19. threw back the bedroom door and stood in the doorway
20. let himself in through the front door

DADWL103 DOORS/WINDOWS/LIGHTS 103 (CLOSING DOORS)

1. closed the door behind him
2. after closing the door carefully he slid the bolt home and slotted in the chain
3. after shutting the door, slipped the bolt automatically and fixed the chain
4. crept out of the room and closed the door silently
5. closing the door behind him with a clatter that echoed in the silence
6. resolutely closed the door behind him
7. ushered her out, then he closed the door firmly behind her
8. shut the door and leaned against it
9. hurled herself at the door and banged it shut, shooting the bolt and putting on the chain
10. putting his hand against the front door, he pushed it closed
11. closed the door carefully and leaned against it
12. ran to the door and dragged it open closing it behind her with a slam
13. pulled her hand from the door latch abruptly and hurled the door shut
14. slammed the door

DADWL104 DOORS/WINDOWS/LIGHTS 104 (KNOCKING ON DOOR)

1. looked up in surprise at the sudden knocking
2. was banging on the door
3. thundered on the door panel with his knuckles

DADWL105 DOORS/WINDOWS/LIGHTS 105 (OPENING A WINDOW)

1. walked over to the window and threw it up

DAED
EATING/DRINKING

DAED101 EATING/DRINKING 101 (COOKING)

1. with shaking hands, filled the kettle, banging it against the taps in her agitation

DAED102 EATING/DRINKING 102 (THE PROCESS OF DRINKING)

1. drained his glasses
2. drank straight from the bottle
3. another glasses followed, tipped down his throat
4. drank the coffee quickly, barely tasting it
5. finished his toast, drained his coffee and stood up
6. sipped thoughtfully from his glasses
7. was about to drink the last of her coffee when lowered the mug again
8. tipped back the goblet and drained it
9. rose and flourished the cup
10. looked down into her coffee mug
11. sipping it with a grimace

12. pushed her plate aside and toyed instead with the glasses of wine
13. took another thoughtful sip from
14. gave up all pretense of eating and reached for her wineglasses
15. raised his glasses slowly
16. raised the cup to her mouth with a shaking hand
17. put down the cup
18. took a sip from his glasses reflectively
19. picked the lemon out of his glasses and sucked it
20. took a sip from his glasses
21. emptied it down in one gulp
22. was drinking hard, the heavy wine bringing a flush of color to his cheekbones
23. sipped her wine, grateful for the warmth it spread through her veins
24. he drank it in a gulp
25. he finished his drink and pushed the glasses back toward her
26. took a deep draught from his glasses
27. raised the cup to her mouth with a awaking hand
28. picked up the whisky glasses, took a couple of gulps from it and put it down
29. drank it quickly and held it out to her again
30. drank it down at a gulp
31. took a sip from his glasses
32. drank quickly
33. had a swig
34. leaned back, sipping the liquid contentedly
35. drank gratefully
36. sucked avidly and liquid filled his mouth
37. it eased the dryness of his mouth
38. picked up his drink and knocked it back
39. raising the teacup to his heavily mustached lips
40. drank in the comfort of his nearness
41. sip gingerly
42. swallow with

43. swallowed eagerly
44. closed his fingers around the glasses and helped guide it to lips
45. sipped the whisky neat
46. drained his glasses
47. took a slug of Scotch
48. nursing her drink
49. took a sip from his glasses reflectively

DAED103 EATING/DRINKING 103 (THE PROCESS OF EATING)

1. finished his toast, drained his coffee and stood up
2. doggedly he picked up his knife and fork
3. turned to the food that had been put down before him
4. pushed back his plate
5. helped her self to a slice of bread
6. pulled her plate toward her
7. put down her knife and fork
8. gave up all pretense of eating and reached for her wineglasses
9. was toying listlessly with her french fries
10. cut into the top of the egg and watched the yolk flow across the plate
11. picked up a sandwich and nibbled on the edge of it
12. munched thoughtfully
13. took a huge mouthful of food
14. took a tentative mouthful of
15. took a large mouthful
16. selected a piece of meat from the plate and chewed it thoughtfully
17. picked up a sandwich and nibbled the edge of it
18. ate with relish
19. fell to eating
20. chomped
21. swallowed eagerly
22. torment was eating at her from inside

23.   picked the lemon out of his glass and sucked it

DAED104 EATING/DRINKING 104 (TOASTING)

1.   raised her glasses innocently
2.   clinked glasses with him amiably

DASW
SLEEPING/WAKING

DASW101 SLEEPING/WAKING 101 (GOING TO SLEEP)

1.   dozing off would invite deeper unconsciousness
2.   suddenly realized that had closed her eyes, giving in to the temptation of sleep
3.   drifting back into the restless, dream-haunted sleep
4.   fell into an uneasy sleep
5.   pulling the covers beneath her chin
6.   succumbing to the numbed sleep of the satisfied lover
7.   sinking deeper into his fog of weariness
8.   whole body was engulfed in tides of weariness
9.   last waking thought before drifted into sleep
10.   lapsed into semi-consciousness from fatigue
11.   turned on his side and willed himself to sleep
12.   fatigue oozed from every pore
13.   slowly her eyelids dropped
14.   forcing her eyes open, made herself stare at it, trying to concentrate on staying awake
15.   relaxed and at peace, turned over and was instantly asleep
16.   fell asleep at last with the bedside lamp on, unable to bring herself to face total darkness
17.   restless turned on her pillow, trying to find a cool spot for her head

18. half hearing noises as drifted further into sleep
19. slid once more into a half-sleeping dream
20. drifted into an uneasy sleep

DASW102 SLEEPING/WAKING 102 (SLEEPING)

1. slept lightly, waking twice in the night to reassure herself that he was still there
2. flung her arm across her closed eyes and shivered before lying still again
3. slept fitfully, half listening for
4. drifting back into wisps of sleep
5. her dreams were attacked
6. sleep had been interrupted periodically by anticipation
7. sinking deeper into his fog of weariness
8. was deeply asleep

DASW103 SLEEPING/WAKING 103 (WAKING UP)

1. pushing away the heavy clogging sleep, struggled to sit up
2. sleep had been interrupted periodically by anticipation
3. dragged herself up out of the fog of sleep
4. eyes still bleary with sleep
5. looked up with an effort
6. with an exclamation of fright sat up, her head swimming
7. fought a groggy disorientation
8. aroused with a start
9. always got up with the face of a bad night
10. like awakening from a deep sleep
11. adjusted to wakefulness
12. aroused herself from the numbness that weighed her down
13. became instantly awake, fully aware of her surroundings
14. became instantly wide awake

15. fought through the cobwebs of night-mare-filled sleep
16. some sixth sense brought her fully aware
17. the misery of the night still haunted her
18. with difficulty struggled back to wakefulness
19. woke suddenly
20. woke very suddenly and lay still, wondering what had heard
21. forcing her eyes open
22. awoke with a start and jolted upright
23. for a moment lay still, her mind a blank, then slowly sat up
24. felt around, her eyes still shut, trying to pull the bedclothes over her again

DAH
RIDING A HORSE

DAH101 RIDING A HORSE 101 (RIDING A HORSE)

1. wheeled his horse and spurred it toward
2. he pulled his horse to a rearing halt, its hooves plunging into the dust
3. his horse stopped of its own accord
4. reined in her horse to a rearing, sweating halt
5. raised her whip and urged her horse into a gallop
6. grabbed at the pommel of her saddle to prevent herself from being thrown
7. sensing fear, the horse plunged suddenly sideways fighting the bit
8. they rode hard, not sparing the horses
9. bent low over his horses' neck
10. let her mare stand for a moment
11. he sent his horse galloping down the ride
12. he pulled his horse to a savage halt, which sent it rearing and plunging sideways
13. groped blindly for his reins
14. stood up in his stirrups

15. bent low over the mare's neck, excited at the prospect of the chase
16. reined it in savagely as it plunged beside the other horses
17. reined in her black mare tightly
18. threw his leg stiffly over the pommel
19. riding very upright
20. helped her into the saddle and then swung himself onto his own horse
21. pulled up her horse
22. pushed the bay into a gallop
23. pulled to a rearing halt
24. they had slowed again to a trot
25. trying to soothe her horse, stroking the sweating neck
26. turned his horse
27. swung himself back up into his saddle
28. picked their way almost dry-shod across the shallows
29. horse shifted restlessly beneath him
30. slid from his saddle, then threw the rein to a groom
31. slid from her horse

DAS
SMOKING

DAS101 SMOKING 101 (SMOKING)

1. he dragged deeply
2. blowing smoke, he followed the trail with his eye
3. ground out his third cigarette into the grass with his heel
4. fumbled in the pocket of his jacket for a pack of cigarettes

FIGURES OF SPEECH

FS1
FORCEFUL

FS1-1 (TRUTHFUL)

1. Candidly declare
2. remark matter-of-factly
3. he spouted out
4. he said evenly
5. dared to talk boldly
6. replied without turning around
7. declared with an innocent openness of spirit
8. declared in deadly earnest
9. admitted quite truthfully
10. groaning with exasperation
11. told him with an open heart
12. said quite pettishly
13. said with unrestrained sincerity
14. was moved to declare
15. admitted lamely

FS1-2 (FORCEFUL)

1. He persevered
2. he said sternly
3. he demanded
4. he urged
5. he shouted
6. he announced
7. he yelled
8. his stentorian voice boomed
9. he bellowed
10. he said sharply
11. he interrupted
12. he screamed
13. he shouted out
14. he said gruffly
15. he said crisply
16. she said harshly

17. he repeated explosively
18. the question was meant to intimidate
19. he said briefly and without detail
20. he said abruptly
21. he said decisively
22. he snarled
23. he warned
24. answer was sharp
25. a clear cold voice
26. dared to talk boldly
27. without raising her voice
28. her voice dominated the room
29. she owned
30. shouted in a leonine roar
31. in a voice edged with burnished steel
32. suggested in a cold hard voice
33. she fairly snorted
34. said in a harder tone of voice
35. she said, not coquettishly
36. she repeated the words to herself
37. he spoke with enormous force, his eyes hardening
38. he repeated his order
39. his tone was insistent
40. his peremptory order cut through her shout

FS1-3 (EXASPERATION)

1. he cried
2. he howled
3. he screamed
4. he spoke impatiently
5. he added savagely
6. with an increasing air of urgency in his voice
7. with childish candor
8. raising her voice for the first time
9. her voice dominated the room
10. replied without turning around

11.   she owned
12.   disclaiming in a mighty voice
13.   shouted in a leonine roar
14.   words were wrested from his lips
15.   shouted with immense pomposity
16.   snapped back pettishly
17.   shouted most abusively in his face
18.   fairly exploded
19.   there was an exaggerated sigh on the other end of the line
20.   words failed her

FS1-4 (UNWILLINGLY)

1.   she said at last unwillingly

FS2
WISHFULL

FS2-1 (WISHFULL)

1.   he said with a sigh
2.   gave a small sigh
3.   he was wishing violently
4.   he said half to himself
5.   with almost a touch of pleading in his voice
6.   a curiously long sigh
7.   he moaned
8.   she cooed like a babe
9.   he sighed grandly
10.   said in a rather whining tone
11.   asked in no little dismay

FS2-2 (WORRIED)

1.   he sighed heavily

2.   he said weakly
3.   he said delicately
4.   she inquired sweetly
5.   sounded genuinely shaken
6.   in a sinking voice
7.   he gave a hollow laugh
8.   he groaned
9.   he asked in a hollow kind of rattle
10.   despondently
11.   he groaned a good deal
12.   said in a tone that seemed to convey a somewhat false composure
13.   said quite regretfully
14.   said in a somewhat pitiful voice
15.   blurted rather sullenly
16.   a pained and mournful voice

FS2-3 (DESPERATION)

1.   he burst out
2.   he added ingenuously
3.   with childlike innocence
4.   he burst out desperately
5.   he droned
6.   he groaned
7.   he wailed
8.   he groaned a good deal
9.   a forthright whine
10.   blurted rather sullenly
11.   asked from the depths of her spirit

FS2-4 (CAUTION)

1.   he said earnestly
2.   he said delicately
3.   she said primly

4.   said somewhat guardedly
5.   fumbling for words

FS3
QUESTIONING

FS3-1 (TALKATIVE)

1.   asked much interested
2.   exhibiting loquacity for the first time
3.   asked in an inanely conversational tone
4.   tried to be idly conversational

FS3-2 (CONVERSATIONAL)

1.   he said with polite concern
2.   asked much interested
3.   exhibiting loquacity for the first time
4.   asked in an inanely conversational tone
5.   tried to be idly conversational

FS3-3 (WONDERING)

1.   he asked incredulously
2.   asked much interested
3.   exclaimed, as if a great discovery had flashed across his mind
4.   he breathed in a solemn half-whisper
5.   asked in some beffudlement
6.   said with a note of sober shyness

FS3-4 (COMPREHENDING)

1.   exclaimed, as if a great discovery had flashed across his mind
2.   he breathed in a solemn half-whisper

3.   admitted grudgingly

FS3-5 (QUESTIONING)

1.   he inquired
2.   he guessed
3.   he asked mildly
4.   said with a distinct note of apprehension
5.   he shouted questions
6.   questions were fired
7.   she asked bitterly
8.   the idle sounding question
9.   the question was meant to intimidate
10.   he asked hoarsely
11.   he queried
12.   he asked irritably
13.   he asked incredulously
14.   he said dubiously
15.   in a voice faint with disbelief
16.   asked much interested
17.   asked somewhat dubiously
18.   asked in an inanely conversational tone
19.   said in a poutish puzzled voice
20.   suggested dubiously
21.   managed to inquire
22.   asked in some beffudlement

FS3-6 (DOUBTFUL)

1.   he said with slight doubt in his voice
2.   he said doubtfully
3.   shaking his head
4.   he said with a distinct note of apprehension
5.   he stopped, confused
6.   he said unsympathetically
7.   she asked bitterly
8.   he protested good-naturedly

9.   he interrupted testily
10. he asked irritably
11. he asked incredulously
12. he said ironically
13. he said dubiously
14. in a voice faint with disbelief
15. asked somewhat dubiously
16. said in a sneering tone
17. he taunted challengingly
18. said in a poutish puzzled voice
19. suggested dubiously
20. said not entirely convincingly
21. snapped with somewhat unconvincing spontaneity

FS3-7 (CONFUSED)

1.   he muttered
2.   shaking his head
3.   he said with a distinct note of apprehension
4.   he stopped, confused
5.   in a poutish puzzled voice
6.   managed to inquire
7.   asked in some beffudlement

FS3-8 (SARCASM)

1.   burned on his lips
2.   was disposed to argue
3.   he said unsympathetically
4.   she asked bitterly
5.   the question was meant to intimidate
6.   he asked irritably
7.   he asked incredulously
8.   his voice edged
9.   on guard
10. he said dubiously
11. in a voice faint with disbelief

12.   she owned in a tone of mock reluctance
13.   asked somewhat dubiously
14.   suggested archly
15.   he said with a great false show of indignation
16.   said in a sneering tone
17.   he taunted challengingly
18.   suggested dubiously
19.   snapped with somewhat unconvincing spontaneity
20.   pointed out fatuously
21.   pointed out dryly
22.   exclaimed rather archly
23.   she flashed back

FS3-9 (ARGUMENTATIVE)

1.   he said with slight doubt in his voice
2.   he said doubtfully
3.   he muttered
4.   shaking his head
5.   he shouted questions
6.   questions were fired
7.   burned on his lips
8.   was disposed to argue
9.   she asked bitterly
10.   the question was meant to intimidate
11.   he protested good-naturedly
12.   he asked hoarsely
13.   humming and huffing
14.   he queried
15.   he interrupted testily
16.   he asked irritably
17.   he asked incredulously
18.   his voice edged
19.   on guard
20.   he said dubiously
21.   in a voice faint with disbelief
22.   she owned in a tone of mock reluctance

23. asked somewhat dubiously
24. suggested archly
25. he said with a great false show of indignation
26. said in a sneering tone
27. he taunted challengingly
28. said in a poutish puzzled voice
29. suggested dubiously
30. said not entirely convincingly
31. snapped with somewhat unconvincing spontaneity
32. pointed out fatuously
33. exclaimed rather archly
34. she was not to be placated

FS3-10 (IRONY)

1. suggested ironically

FS3-11 (TESTY)

1. he said unsympathetically
2. she asked bitterly   he asked hoarsely
3. he muttered
4. humming and huffing
5. burned on his lips
6. he interrupted testily
7. he asked irritably
8. his voice edged
9. on guard
10. he said dubiously
11. in a voice faint with disbelief
12. she owned in a tone of mock reluctance
13. asked somewhat dubiously
14. suggested archly
15. he said with a great false show of indignation
16. said in a sneering tone
17. said not entirely convincingly
18. snapped with somewhat unconvincing spontaneity

19. pointed out fatuously
20. pointed out dryly
21. exclaimed rather archly

FS3-12 (SHOCK)

1. he shouted questions
2. he stopped, confused
3. he asked hoarsely
4. he asked incredulously
5. voice faint with disbelief
6. he said with a great false show of indignation
7. said, slightly aghast in a moral sense

FS313 (INCOMPREHENSION)

1. slowly sank into mutual incomprehension as they tried to find some common ground

FS4
NERVOUS

FS4-1 (NERVOUS)

1. he stammered
2. he said lamely
3. he spluttered
4. he coughed   he said weakly
5. he said worriedly
6. he asked anxiously
7. he offered weakly
8. he stammered, amazed
9. he said huskily
10. he blurted out
11. his voice trailed away uneasily
12. he swallowed

13. he merely nodded, not trusting his voice
14. he managed to say
15. her voice was raised
16. her voice was pitched low and breathless
17. he asked hoarsely
18. he was talking nonsense
19. he spoke with difficulty
20. he said nervously, keeping his voice low
21. he said worriedly
22. he said shakily
23. forced a nervous laugh
24. she whispered
25. his voice trembling a little
26. in a voice not exactly without a tremolo
27. agreed tremulously

FS4-2 (POLITENESS)

1. he inquired
2. he said with polite concern
3. he asked mildly   the idle sounding question
4. he protested good-naturedly
5. he queried
6. he said carefully
7. asked much interested
8. tried to be idly conversational
9. with thin-drawn politeness

FS4-3 (RELIEF)

1. a sigh fled
2. he breathed a sigh of relief
3. sighed with relief
4. his voice weak with relief
5. he was relieved
6. with a momentary sigh of relief
7. fairly moaned in relief

8.   with a great relenting sigh
9.   she had been prepared for a standup argument

FS4-4 (TENSION)

1.   he blurted out
2.   he merely nodded, not trusting his voice
3.   he said through shut teeth
4.   her voice was raised
5.   her voice was pitched low and breathless
6.   she said with forced calm
7.   he spoke with difficulty
8.   he trod carefully
9.   he talked sparingly
10.   he said tightly
11.   he hissed
12.   almost shouted
13.   trying to keep his voice level
14.   he sucked in his breath
15.   his voice low and strained
16.   his voice going up a scale as he said
17.   he said in rather a quiet voice
18.   said in a much tinier voice
19.   replied with some vexation
20.   his voice had suddenly lost its lightness
21.   there was an edge to his voice

FS4-5 (SECRETIVE)

1.   he lowered his voice still further
2.   his voice was laconic
3.   she spoke in a stage whisper, designed to be heard by everyone in the room

FS4-6 (FEARFUL)

1.   he said lamely

2. he spluttered
3. gasped in alarm
4. he said weakly
5. he said worriedly
6. he asked anxiously
7. he offered weakly
8. he cried aghast
9. she said with patent fear
10. he said huskily
11. he answered as meekly as a girl
12. his voice trailed away uneasily
13. he asked hoarsely
14. he said in a suppressed voice
15. scream was choked back
16. strangled gasp
17. breathing ragged
18. voice shaking
19. he spoke with difficulty
20. he said aghast
21. he dropped his voice
22. he said limply
23. he said shakily
24. trying to keep his voice level
25. he sucked in his breath
26. his voice quavered slightly
27. his voice going up a scale as he said
28. his whisper hardly rose above a rasp
29. gabbled the words wildly
30. he yelped
31. a gasp of stunned horror
32. returned with a shudder
33. shouting in a frenzy
34. he blathered on
35. said in a much tinier voice
36. stammered in no little trepidation
37. cried in no little terror
38. exclaimed in alarm and dismay

39. must have shouted wordlessly
40. she broke off with a little cry
41. her reply was scarcely audible

FS5
HUMOR

FS5-1 (HUMOR)

1. he chuckled slightly
2. he said cheerfully
3. he roared with laughter
4. he chuckled to himself
5. with a quiet humor coloring his tone
6. she smiled a little at
7. a warm note of amusement in her tone
8. said japingly

FS5-2 (HUMORING)

1. amusement veiling contempt
2. he said indulgently
3. he said patiently
4. he said with a wink
5. he said blandly
6. sounding fatherly
7. he agreed dryly
8. she said soothingly
9. she smiled tolerantly
10. chided in an avuncular tone
11. put in gently

FS5-3 (FUN)

1. murmured mischievously

FS5-4 (LAUGHTER)

1.   a bellowing laugh
2.   he was convulsed with laughter
3.   his laugh was rich
4.   he roared
5.   huge waves of laughter
6.   a fit of laughter caught him
7.   he chuckled slightly
8.   he said cheerfully
9.   he roared with laughter
10.   he chuckled to himself
11.   his laughter boomed
12.   barked a laugh
13.   a ripple of laughter in his voice
14.   a high, loud laugh
15.   he laughed to himself
16.   his laugh was brittle
17.   he said through the laughter
18.   he broke into hysterical laughter
19.   he laughed agreement
20.   smiled wryly   he burst out laughing
21.   sounded suspiciously like a snicker
22.   she tittered
23.   gurgled chirpily
24.   she hooted
25.   with a low chuckle of amusement
26.   observed with a laugh
27.   laughed decorously
28.   suppressed a gurgle of laughter
29.   a hollow laugh
30.   laughing uproariously
31.   breaking into raucous and ironic laughter
32.   broke into braying laughter
33.   a strange gurgling sound halfway between a cough and a laugh
34.   a fine breaker of laughter
35.   roar of ribald laughter

36. softened her anger with a little laugh
37. broke into callow giggles
38. laughing rather unconvincingly
39. laughed good-naturedly
40. declared with a little laugh
41. rocking with silent laughter
42. a thread of laughter in his voice
43. he laughed exultantly

FS5-5 (GRIMLY HUMOUROUS)

1. he added wryly
2. with forced joviality

FS6
SURPRISE

FS6-1 (GUILT)

1. he winced
2. demanded with guilt-driven stridency

FS6-2 (CONFUSION)

1. she asked bewildered
2. he was puzzled
3. he said stupefied
4. he was bewildered
5. he asked flabbergasted
6. he seemed a little taken aback
7. in sheer bewilderment
8. suggested in a peculiar voice that seemed somehow befuddled at it's own existence
9. said in perfect befuddlement
10. he asked blankly
11. she whispered between her fingers

FS6-3 (SURPRISE)

1. there was a moment's astonished silence
2. he said incredulously
3. he choked
4. he exclaimed
5. he yelped   he said, rather startled
6. he said, slightly taken aback
7. he whispered in astonishment
8. his voice was a strangled gurgle
9. she sounded considerably startled
10. expressed surprise
11. he said astonished
12. he gasped
13. he seemed a little taken aback
14. he said, a little nonplused
15. in breathless amazement
16. exclaimed in great surprise
17. he declared more in genuine amazement than pique
18. exclaimed in utter wonderment
19. she had been prepared for a standup argument

FS6-4 (SHOCK)

1. he practically choked
2. shocked into bluntness
3. he said shocked
4. he asked flabbergasted
5. he said appalled
6. he said thunderstruck
7. he said awed
8. she exclaimed, shocked
9. with a gasp in his voice
10. uttered a wild cry

11. was rendered speechless
12. exclaimed in horror and outrage

FS7
A BREAK IN SPEECH

FS7-1 (A PAUSE)

1. but only silence answered her
2. there was a moment's astonished silence
3. he paused
4. he tried to form the words
5. he coughed politely
6. his voice trailed off
7. he cleared his throat
8. pause for a moment's reflection
9. he pondered
10. he considered for a moment
11. he rolled the word around
12. he hesitated
13. he paused uncertainly
14. she interrupted
15. he seemed to be waiting for an answer
16. his voice trailed away
17. she paused on the lie
18. for a shrinking moment he paused
19. he held his tongue
20. he swallowed the words
21. he stopped confused
22. a startled pause
23. he reflected
24. at a loss for words
25. made no immediate reply
26. he thought a moment
27. he hesitated

28. did not quite know how to put it
29. made a mental note
30. just enough of a pause
31. an insulting pause
32. an unhurried pause
33. he thought a moment
34. paused for a breath
35. the words hung
36. there was a pause
37. the conversation ceased
38. enough of a pause to make a point
39. he pondered
40. as his murmur of words died away
41. he had to stop and work out his words
42. he had to regain discipline over his voice
43. a nasty hush descended
44. he paused and maneuvered his thoughts
45. lapsed into silence
46. he left a longish pause
47. the pause had become embarrassing enough
48. considered this for a moment
49. for a long moment she hesitated
50. regarded in arch silence for a moment
51. rolled it around the palate of his mind
52. it was a long while before she summoned the composure to speak
53. she cut herself off in mid sentence
54. a long and quite uncharacteristic silence
55. she hesitated again, suddenly embarrassed
56. he waited for her to say more
57. words failed her
58. she broke off with a little cry
59. she stopped short, groping for a name
60. she stopped abruptly
61. there was a long pause as they looked warily at one another

1.   he continued
2.   he added
3.   he began
4.   he said finally
5.   after a significant pause
6.   he said at last
7.   he confirmed
8.   he added on further reflection
9.   after a moment he replied
10. at length she spoke
11. he said at length
12. interrupted with a flood of words
13. breaking the silence
14. after a moment's reflection
15. he added under his breath
16. said as an afterthought
17. broke the short silence
18. after a very tiny pause
19. he went on to say
20. in a sudden blurt of coherence
21. after a slight wondering pause
22. with a new tone in his voice
23. continued in a lighter tone
24. after considering
25. said at length
26. went on matter-of-factly
27. at last deigned to utter
28. it was a long while before she summoned the composure to speak
29. finally managed to whisper
30. called out at length
31. at last she found her tongue
32. broke in after a long and quite uncharacteristic silence
33. said in a similar vein
34. she found herself saying

35. he shifted casually into
36. she said at last unwillingly
37. she went on with a heavy sigh
38. she went on without turning
39. shaking his head, he recovered himself with an effort
40. she said after a moment's hesitation
41. she continued, irritated
42. she whispered at last
43. she went on after a moment
44. she said at last

FS7-3 (CHANGING THE SUBJECT)

1. his tone changed

FS7-4 (PURSUING THE SUBJECT FUTHER)

1. she refused to be distracted
2. she continued, irritated
3. he prompted at last

FS8
SOLEMNITY

FS8-1 (SOLEMNITY)

1. he said solemnly
2. he said quietly
3. said gravely
4. he whispered
5. he intoned
6. he said majestically
7. he said thoughtfully
8. he said softly
9. he spoke with respectful formality
10. with sweet humility
11. said gravely

12.   said tonelessly
13.   he said heavily
14.   she said with a heavy sigh

FS8-2 (APOLOGETIC)

1.   said in an almost apologetic tone

FS8-3 (PITY)

1.   he said gently
2.   he said with sympathy
3.   he said indulgently
4.   he said, not unkindly
5.   he said compassionately
6.   he said, deep with pity
7.   she said with sympathetic softness

FS8-4 (SADNESS)

1.   he said heavily
2.   said in a flat dull voice
3.   muttered in an uninflected monotone
4.   muttered unhappily

FS8-5 (CALMNESS)

1.   he said gently
2.   he said quietly
3.   he said slowly
4.   he said with control
5.   he said mildly
6.   he patiently explained
7.   he said with infinite calmness
8.   he said soothingly
9.   he said perfectly calmly
10.   he did not raise to the bait

11.   voice was hauntingly calm
12.   replied in a tone of infuriating tranquility
13.   in a smug tone of tranquil sweetness
14.   said in a strong tranquil voice

FS8-6 (CLEARLY UNDERSTOOD)

1.   he said lucidly
2.   he said simply
3.   he spoke with patent honesty he spoke frankly
4.   he said matter-of-factly
5.   she said, not facetiously

FS9
CONTENT/DISCONTENT

FS9-1 (APPROVAL)

1.   murmured approval
2.   made no further objection
3.   agreed sourly
4.   exclaimed approvingly
5.   said more conversationally
6.   exclaimed in forthright admiration

FS9-2 (CONTENT)

1.   said with satisfaction
2.   he said agreeably
3.   a long smiling sigh
4.   said airily
5.   said with a suppressed sigh
6.   remarked in a pleased tone
7.   replied, well pleased
8.   they hardly spoke at all as they walked

9.   asked lazily in the silence

FS9-3 (DISCONTENT)

1.   he muttered
2.   he said with unconcealed contempt
3.   explained angrily
4.   exclaimed in irritation
5.   he said petulantly
6.   he demanded
7.   he said acidly
8.   he said coldly
9.   he protested
10.   he said with contempt
11.   with a touch of impatience
12.   she told him sourly
13.   she tut-tutted
14.   he said dryly
15.   he thought with savage irritation
16.   her voice full of scorn
17.   she said bitterly
18.   he bristled
19.   he spoke rudely
20.   he snapped
21.   he said with open contempt
22.   barely concealed irritation
23.   he complained loudly
24.   he shouted for vengeance
25.   he spat
26.   he said exasperated
27.   he said sarcastically
28.   he said coldly
29.   he said impatiently
30.   he asked abruptly
31.   he groaned wearily
32.   said tartly

33.   he said grumpily
34.   he said testily
35.   he asked with growing frustration
36.   he asked, not entirely pleased
37.   he said ruefully
38.   he grumbled
39.   half-articulated protests
40.   said in a surly tone
41.   in a tone of indignant protest
42.   speaking in a sulky tone of voice
43.   replied in a gloomy voice
44.   agreed sourly
45.   coiling for the pounce
46.   said with less than enthusiasm
47.   he muttered sourly
48.   said crossly
49.   was reproachful

FS9-4 (INDIFFERENCE)

1.   he said carelessly
2.   she said in an emotionless voice
3.   she sounded completely indifferent
4.   he merely laughed
5.   he wondered idly
6.   spoke with indifference
7.   she said distantly
8.   he yawned as he spoke
9.   said absently
10.   he said with studied negligence
11.   his voice suddenly flat
12.   he grunted noncommittally
13.   gave a little grunt
14.   she was too tired to argue anymore

FS9-5 (NEUTRAL)

1. his voice was carefully neutral
2. voice was curiously flat

FS10
COMMANDING

FS10-1 (DIGNIFIED)

1. he spoke with disconcerting self-possession
2. a kind of professional sincerity
3. he said with tendentious gravity
4. said in a firm but respectful voice

FS10-2 (ASSURANCE)

1. he said firmly
2. he spoke with confidence
3. he said easily
4. he declared extravagantly
5. declared grandly

FS10-3 (COMMANDING)

1. he called
2. he demanded
3. he said haughtily
4. he insisted
5. he bawled
6. he warned
7. his stentorian voice boomed
8. he spoke sharply, authoritatively
9. he assumed
10. he was arrogantly curt
11. swiftly commanded
12. he barked
13. he grunted

14. tried to make the words sound important
15. he said curtly
16. he threw an order over his shoulder
17. an imperious voice ordered
18. he said with harsh abruptness
19. his voice boomed hollowly
20. quiet authoritative drawl
21. he said all too-knowingly

FS10-4 (AGREEMENT)

1. she acquiesced
2. she agreed thoughtfully
3. he made a sort of grumping noise
4. readily enough agreed
5. assured her blithely
6. was forced to admit
7. was forced to own
8. abruptly she capitulated

FS10-5 (SUBSERVIENT)

1. he repeated obediently
2. she acquiesced
3. with an unaccustomed note of humility
4. he responded weakly
5. she swallowed the automatic flare-up of rebellion

FS11
PRIDE

FS11-1 (PRIDE)

1. he said proudly
2. he snorted
3. cried out triumphantly

4.   with an air of much pride
5.   asserted with evident pride

FS11-2 (EMBARRASSMENT)

1.   she said in embarrassment
2.   he cried
3.   he said with sudden realization
4.   he said gruffly
5.   he said hesitating
6.   he spoke lamely
7.   he began indignantly
8.   began to speak haltingly
9.   with an attempt at lightness
10.   his reply was too quick
11.   he croaked helplessly
12.   he heard himself say
13.   hesitantly at first

FS12
HOPELESS

FS12-1 (HURT)

1.   he wailed
2.   he began desperately
3.   he said tersely
4.   whined in an injured tone
5.   said with a sob
6.   spoke rustily
7.   in an injured tone
8.   fairly whined

FS12-2 (SORROWFUL)

1.   he wailed
2.   he said dejectedly
3.   she said heavily
4.   the words came heavily
5.   he said brokenly
6.   he said unhappily
7.   remarked with a sign of regret
8.   said, shaking her head thoughtfully
9.   he said with a sob
10.   whispered forlornly

FS12-3 (HOPELESSNESS)

1.   she said in an emotionless voice
2.   he started hopelessly
3.   his voice, a thread of hoarse sound
4.   she said heavily
5.   he said flatly
6.   the words came heavily
7.   he said woodenly
8.   a dead voice
9.   his voice was flat
10.   made the automatic response
11.   he said helplessly
12.   in a sad and depressed voice
13.   muttered bleakly
14.   with a sinking heart

FS12-4 (TIREDLY)

1.   he said blearily
2.   he said tiredly
3.   she said heavily
4.   the words came heavily
5.   a dead voice
6.   he said wearily

7.   said with an uncharacteristic lack of energy

FS12-5 (DISAPPOINTMENT)

1.   he laughed brittley
2.   he asked hoarsely
3.   he said thinly
4.   he said brokenly
5.   in a tone of disappointment
6.   fairly whined
7.   she said with adult bitterness

FS13
MALEVOLENT

FS13-1 (MALEVOLENT)

1.   he said not entirely reassuringly
2.   he said with unconcealed contempt
3.   explained angrily
4.   he said with an evil grin
5.   he said, all the charm vanishing from his voice
6.   he added nastily
7.   she said with shrill malice
8.   a weighty warning
9.   uncanny laughter
10.   the venom in his voice
11.   he said balefully
12.   he said venomously
13.   he hissed
14.   laughed insanely
15.   he said silkily
16.   laughed obscenely
17.   bellowing as if challenging
18.   gave a bark of humor lacking laughter
19.   laugh had no humor in it   he said with muted savagery
20.   a little giggle of evil satisfaction

21. a wicked laugh
22. he sniggered
23. smiled sickeningly
24. he answered in a kind of growl
25. fairly snarled   said in a tone of poisonous sweetness
26. he said threateningly
27. his tone was becoming threatening
28. his tone had been full of venom

FS13-2 (DISGUST)

1. he said with scorn
2. her lip curled
3. he said dryly
4. he said with contempt
5. said with distaste
6. he said, half nauseated
7. he snorted derisively
8. exclaimed with a shudder
9. he shrugged in scorn at
10. a heckling remark formed upon his lips
11. choked back her disgust and anger
12. she exclaimed in disgust after a moment

FS13-3 (ANGER)

1. He said furiously
2. exclaimed in outrage
3. he cried
4. he howled
5. he wailed
6. he made the situation plain
7. a savage war cry
8. she flared into anger
9. angry spitting voice
10. he went on without prompting
11. he said with fierce self-control

12.   he said narrowly
13.   he said harshly
14.   he said relentlessly
15.   he said grimly
16.   he said, a little louder than necessary
17.   he exploded
18.   he picked the word delicately
19.   with a thinness to his voice
20.   he said irritatedly
21.   he yelled
22.   he bellowed   he said caustically
23.   the words were sudden-raw
24.   his words like bullets
25.   with a hoarse bellowing
26.   with a cry of pure rage
27.   he almost spat
28.   her voice cracked with rage
29.   broke in shrilly
30.   screamed at the top of her voice
31.   exclaimed with no little pique
32.   exclaimed in wounded anger
33.   full throated voice of wounded outrage
34.   a tone of angry dejection
35.   fairly bellowing her outrage
36.   all but bellowed
37.   she flashed back
38.   he cursed quietly
39.   he barked
40.   said quietly, trying resolutely to keep her temper
41.   she swore under her breath

FS13-4 (RUDE)

1.   his voice was laconic
2.   he barked

FS14
EXCITEMENT

FS14-1 (EXCITEMENT)

1. breathless excitement
2. he cried
3. wild cheers broke out
4. he erupted
5. he breathed
6. he squirmed
7. he gasped
8. talking eagerly and excitedly together with much gesture
9. he chimed in
10. he said with sudden excitement
11. she whispered in pleased excitement
12. he spoke impulsively
13. he burst out irresistibly
14. buzz of talk
15. a yell of exultation put in eagerly
16. he said in triumph
17. was jabbering excitedly
18. he panted
19. burned on his lips
20. he said earnestly
21. he said eagerly
22. spoke with uncontrolled emotion
23. found himself shouting farewells excitedly
24. he blurted
25. he choked out
26. it was hard to talk
27. his saliva almost choking him
28. he said breathlessly
29. he said tightly
30. he said, fighting for control he said in a rush
31. he rounded abruptly upon
32. there was a slight catch in her voice

33. he burst forth
34. in a thick intense whisper
35. burst into a torrent of speech
36. said with no little enthusiasm
37. was moved to enthusiastically declare
38. sang out, with enthusiasm
39. said with such a guileless and pretty enthusiasm
40. brimming with enthusiasm
41. burst forth into a prophetic strain
42. burst out into acclamations
43. exclaimed in a wild, mad rush
44. in a rush of fervent feeling, she cried
45. began in a torrent of speech
46. a perfect torrent choked in my throat
47. he articulated rather breathlessly
48. breathlessly gasped out
49. declared to him breathlessly, as if she could absolutely guarantee it
50. speaking low, and half-breathlessly
51. laughing rather breathlessly
52. eagerly and breathlessly uttered, without break or pause
53. able to speak for emotion
54. said slowly and with emotion
55. he said in a choked voice
56. her voice was lively, animated
57. talking rapidly, musically
58. speaking with exceptionally correct articulation
59. tried to say something, but he could not utter it
60. he cried in a shrill voice
61. she said in a voice breaking with emotion
62. lips quivered with emotion as she answered
63. in a voice choking with incoherent words
64. he said aloud, as one does under powerful impressions
65. his voice indicating a suppressed emotion
66. cried in a boyish voice, trembling with emotion
67. voice was rising in intensity
68. he began with extreme emotion

69. in a voice thrilled with emotion
70. cried out with a thundering voice
71. shaking with emotion, his first phrases were even unintelligible
72. could hardly speak clearly
73. his voice testifying emotion
74. she mastered herself, controlled the spasm in her throat
75. hardly able to utter the words for emotion
76. she murmured, almost livid with emotion
77. taken so much by surprise as to betray more emotion than usual
78. uttered with deep emotion
79. he made no disguise of his emotion
80. in tones so broken with emotion that often he had to pause
81. with a half-suppressed gasp of emotion
82. she checked emotion, and said in her low, firm voice
83. in a voice of which he vainly tried to conceal the emotion
84. raised a shrill voice
85. pronounced by a voice full of emotion
86. instantly showed much amiable emotion, and said
87. gulping down a very bitter emotion
88. the tone seemed to gush up out of the deep well of her heart
89. he spoke with relish
90. with an inarticulate exclamation
91. a loud cry of surprise escaped my lips
92. his voice began to rise
93. his voice, trembling, vibrant with emotion
94. at that stage of emotion in which one does not speak for fear of weeping
95. she broke in with excitement
96. said the woman, in an imperative voice
97. calling them with a screech like a peacock
98. he eagerly declared
99. with an earnest shout
100. reverently exclaimed

FS14-2 (ROMANTIC EXCITEMENT)

1. her voice throbbed
2. he said huskily
3. he asked hoarsely
4. he spoke with uncontrolled emotion
5. mumbling incomprehensibly
6. putting on a low husky voice
7. there was a slight catch in her voice
8. sighed throatily
9. an honest sensual moan
10. he purred dreamily
11. he said with a certain lack of focus
12. replied throatily
13. cooing softly in his ear

FS15
JOYFUL

FS15-1 (FRIENDLY)

1. her voice was honey sweet
2. a smile sounded in his voice
3. he said grinning
4. he said genially

FS15-2 (AFFECTION)

1. said with unconcealed affection

FS15-3 (CONTENTEDNESS)

1. he was never tired of telling
2. he said luxuriously

3.	he said triumphantly
4.	he said well pleased
5.	chuckling gleefully

FS15-4 (JOYFULL)

1.	he chimed in
2.	she gave a little laugh
3.	he said cheerfully
4.	she laughed aloud
5.	he said happily
6.	talking gaily
7.	laughed under his breath
8.	lilting speech
9.	rich laugh
10.	bubbled with laughter
11.	exploding with sudden laughter
12.	broke into laughter
13.	a light easy laugh
14.	she piped in cheerily
15.	shouts of glee
16.	in joyous tones
17.	in a glad voice
18.	replied, brightening at
19.	crying in pure happiness
20.	broke into delighted laughter
21.	she burbled
22.	a great whooping laugh
23.	said with unholy gleefulness
24.	he laughed, a happy musical sound
25.	laughed sweetly
26.	said almost gaily
27.	she chortled
28.	obviously enjoying herself immensely
29.	piped up brightly
30.	declared to a cleansing burst of laughter
31.	cheerful in her chatter

32.   she let out a little cry of pleasure

FS15-5 (KINDNESS)

1.   she said with rough kindliness

FS15-6 (COMFORTING)

1.   said in a sympathetic tone
2.   in a gentle tone
3.   he muttered fatuously

FS16
GREETINGS

FS16-1 (GREETINGS)

1.   he hailed softly
2.   a word of courtesy
3.   greeted him amiably
4.   he called out quietly
5.   he smiled a welcome
6.   he called grandly called out a friendly greeting

FS16-2 (SUMMONS)

1.   he whistled a bird call
2.   he gave a queer whistle

FS16-3 (FAREWELLS)

1.   he nodded farewell

EMOTIONS

E1
FORCEFUL

E1-1 (TRUTHFUL)

    1.   heartbreaking sincerity

E1-2 (FORCEFUL)

    1.   quelled an urge
    2.   the remembrance he felt startled him

E1-3 (INTENSE)

    1.   praying with a faith suddenly so intense, so absolute, that it filled her with a calm certainty that her prayers would be heard
    2.   the urge to go down on her knees and then cross herself was like a primeval hangover of some strange superstition

E2
WISHFUL

E2-1 (WISHFUL)

    1.   feeling a long forgotten urge

E2-2 (WORRIED)

    1.   a pang of worry

E2-3 (DESPERATION)

    1.   almost ruptured by desire
    2.   a frenzy of despair

E2-4 (CAUTION)

1.   tensely expected to be disappointed
2.   caution kept him aloof

E3
QUESTIONING

E3-1 (WONDERING)

1.   deep in formless thought

E3-2 (QUESTIONING)

1.   her mind rang bells of warning
2.   a little thought decided him not to

E3-4 (ARGUMENTATIVE)

1.   she was not to be placated

E4
NERVOUS

E4-1 (NERVOUS)

1.   a horror-chill rushed into his hear
2.   felt an enormous weight off his mind
3.   his stomach felt empty
4.   his sweat chilled
5.   filled with nausea
6.   he was poised between life and death
7.   his mind worked frantically
8.   his stomach turned over
9.   his heart missed a beat
10.   felt the inner terror
11.   fluttering with fear   fog of terror

12. fear washed away his strength
13. brinked on insanity
14. dissolved his spine
15. scared wild
16. sudden nip of fear
17. relaxed a fraction of his
18. tenseness went out of him
19. willing each muscle to relax
20. he jammed the brake on his line of thought
21. nasty creepy feeling
22. every part of him screaming
23. clotted with horror
24. filled with a terrible fear
25. heart beat a little faster than usual
26. set his pulses to pounding
27. frightened to the point of collapse
28. chill entered his bones
29. a state of numb dread
30. set the spirit shivering
31. n icy hand round her heart
32. felt as if her psyche had been rung by a mallet

E4-2 (FEARFUL)

1. the urge to go down on her knees and then cross herself was like a primeval hangover of some strange superstition
2. somewhere a shadow had moved in the back of her mind, and she felt a flicker of warning her heart in her mouth

E4-3 (SELFCONSCIOUS)

1. conscious of the eyes that were all focused on her
2. she could feel their eyes uncomfortably on her back

E5
HUMOR

E5-1 (HUMOR)

1.   his amusement was vast
2.   more fun than a box full of kittens

E6
SURPRISE

E6-1 (SURPRISE)

1.   a flicker of surprise
2.   a quiver with amazement
3.   beyond his exhausted comprehension
4.   fighting for room in his head
5.   his head went a little swimmy
6.   a few moments of pure thoughtless shock

E6-2 (SHOCK)

1.   not believing she had seen right
2.   was not disturbed
3.   deep in remorse
4.   a serenity that flowed from her
5.   a cool, even temper
6.   his thought was crystalline-calm
7.   with absentminded queenliness

E7
SOLEMNITY

E7-1 (CALMNESS)

1.   praying with a faith suddenly so intense, so absolute, that it had filled her with a calm certainty that her prayers would be heard

---

2.   determined not to be put out

E8
DISCONTENT

E8-1 (PATIENT)

1.   trying resolutely to keep her temper

E8-2 (DISCONTENT)

1.   boiling with envy
2.   his soul twisted uneasily
3.   the bitterness began to well
4.   hard to stomach
5.   he stifled a curse
6.   sick of the cat and mouse game
7.   tried to hide the bitterness
8.   angry in spite of himself
9.   uncharacteristically short-tempered quiet patience
10.   held firmly to the rags of his temper
11.   air of disdainful indifference
12.   churlish ingratitude

E8-3 (INDIFFERENCE)

1.   ignoring her with calculated disdain

E9
COMMANDING

E9-1 (DIGNIFIED)

1.   dignified and demure as a queen

E9-2 (ASSURANCE)

1.   praying with a faith suddenly so intense, so absolute, that it had filled her with a calm certainty that her prayers would be hers

E9-3 (RESOLVE)

1.   something grew coldly determined inside of her
2.   she took a grip on herself
3.   determined not to be put out

E10
PRIDE

E10-1 (PRIDE)

1.   tried not to let his pride show
2.   he was something of a dandy

E10-2 (EMBARASSMENT)

1.   spiced with the bile of shame
2.   He felt seedy
3.   difficult to speak
4.   feeling suddenly guilty
5.   his composure suddenly shattered
6.   wet with embarrassment
7.   he felt naked
8.   covering his embarrassment
9.   raw with embarrassment
10.   hating himself for his outburst
11.   shyly tried to cover
12.   he felt suddenly hot
13.   a twinge of embarrassment

E11

HOPELESS

E11-1 (HOPELESSNESS)

1. forced his brain to work
2. exquisite agony
3. his heart sank
4. shadow of dismay
5. a knife in his heart
6. bleeding inside
7. something very close to real heartbreak
8. little packets of grief
9. he was feeling solemn and joyless
10. stomach dropped in gross dismay
11. empty of spirit

E11-2 (LONELINESS)
1. she ached with loneliness

E11-3 (MISERY)

1. a quick pang of misery

E12
MALEVOLENT

E12-1 (MALEVOLENT)

1. his rage snapped
2. he felt squeamish
3. delicately suppressed aversion
4. hot anger
5. a violent distaste for
6. tremble with anger
7. formless sullen anger
8. sent an adrenal tide boiling through his blood

E12-2 (ANGER)

1. could feel herself shaking with anger
2. felt a sudden surge of anger flow through him
3. her fear eclipsed by a wave of scorn and fury
4. she was furiously indignant

E13
EXCITEMENT

E13-1 (EXCITEMENT)

1. a wild idea began to flower in his mind
2. he controlled his excitement
3. his mind racing
4. brain churned with excitement
5. his feathers ruffled
6. his mind was alive
7. warmed by the touch
8. vivid in his thoughts
9. his eager mind
10. alive in every fiber
11. a sort of excited waiting
12. excitement burned inside of him
13. tingling going up and down his spine
14. hungry for new excitement
15. a frission of excitement went through
16. charisma-drunken awe
17. alive with meaning
18. slow and smoky ecstasy
19. thoughtless and mindless appreciation
20. wild heights of abandonment

E14
JOYFUL

E14-1 (AFFECTION)

1.　　felt a rush of warm emotion

E14-2 (CONTENTEDNESS)

1.　　she felt absolutely at peace

E14-3 (JOYFULL)

1.　　relaxing contentedly
2.　　laugh came from inside
3.　　it warmed him it did his heart good
4.　　his feet hardly touching the ground
5.　　shouting with laughter inside
6.　　take comfort where you can find it
7.　　familiar as an old flannel shirt
8.　　friendlier than a wet bird dog
9.　　warm deep inside
10.　　a curious kind of manic joy
11.　　blissed out haze
12.　　irrationally happy

E14-4 (TRUST)

1.　　she could feel herself drifting willingly under his spell

E14-5 (LONGING/DESIRE)

1.　　she could feel the longing that stretched like a thong
　　　between them
2.　　naked longing
3.　　worn out with longing

E15
FEAR

E15-1 (FEAR)

1.   she felt herself go rigid

E15-2 (PANIC)

1.   she had been consumed with panic
2.   trying to ignore her increasing panic
3.   panic-stricken
4.   overwhelmed with panic

MOVING PARTS
"PHYSICAL DESCRIPTIONS OF BODY PART MOVEMENTS"
INDEX

SHOULDERS
SH101 SHOULDERS 101 – PAGE 6
SH102 SHOULDERS 102 (SHIVERING – PAGE 6
SH103 SHOULDERS 103 (GESTURING WITH SHOULDER) – PAGE 6
SH104 SHOULDERS 104 (TOUCHING) – PAGE 7
SH105 SHOULDERS 105 (SUPPORTING SOMETHING) – PAGE 9
SH106 SHOULDERS 106 (SHOULDER BLADES) – PAGE 10
SH107 SHOULDERS 107 (PAIN) – PAGE 10
SH108 SHOULDERS 108 (STRAIGHTENING SHOULDERS) – PAGE 10
SH109 SHOULDERS 109 (MOVING THE SHOULDERS) – PAGE 11
SH110 SHOULDERS 110 (KISSING SHOULDERS) – PAGE 11
SH111 SHOULDERS 111 (LOOKING OVER SHOULDER) – PAGE 11
SH112 SHOULDERS 112 (STRETCHING) – PAGE 12
SH113 SHOULDERS 113 (USING SHOULDERS) – PAGE 12
SH114 SHOULDERS 114 (PROTECTING SHOULDERS) – PAGE 12
SH115 SHOULDERS 115 (SLOUCHING) – PAGE 12
SH116 SHOULDERS 116 (FEELING SENSATIONS) – PAGE 12

CHEST
CS101 CHEST 101 – PAGE 13
CS102 CHEST 102 (TIGHTNESS IN CHEST) – PAGE 13
CS103 CHEST 103 (CHEST EXPANDING) – PAGE 13
CS104 CHEST 104 (TOUCHING CHEST) – PAGE 14
CS105 CHEST 105 (CHEST HAIR) – PAGE 14
CS106 CHEST 106 (HEAVINESS IN CHEST) – PAGE 14
CS107 CHEST 107 (CHEST MOVING) – PAGE 14
CS108 CHEST 108 (SUPPORTING SOMETHING) – PAGE 14
CS109 CHEST 109 (CHEST TO CHEST OR BREAST) – PAGE 14
CS110 CHEST 110 (EXPOSING CHEST) – PAGE 15
CS111 CHEST 111 (FEELING SENSATIONS) – PAGE 15
CS112 CHEST 112 (PAIN IN CHEST) – PAGE 15

BREAST
BS101 BREAST 101 – PAGE 15
BS102 BREAST 102 (TOUCHING) – PAGE 15
BS103 BREAST 103 (FEELING SENSATIONS) – PAGE 17
BS104 BREAST 104 (RESPONDING TO STIMULI) – PAGE 17
BS105 BREAST 105 (MOVING) – PAGE 18
BS106 BREAST 106 (KISSING BREASTS) – PAGE 18
BS107 BREAST 107 (EXPOSING BREAST) – PAGE 19
BS108 BREAST 108 (SUPPORTING SOMETHING) – PAGE 19
BS109 BREAST 109 (COVERING BREAST) – PAGE 19

BS110 BREAST 110 (LACTATING) – PAGE 19
BS111 BREAST 111 (LOOKING AT BREASTS) – PAGE 20

RIBS
RB101 RIBS 101 – PAGE 20
RB102 RIBS 102 (RIBS MOVING) – PAGE 20
RB103 RIBS 103 (TOUCHING RIBS) – PAGE 20
RB104 RIBS 104 (FEELING CONSTRAINED) – PAGE 20

LUNGS
LN101 LUNGS 101 – PAGE 21

HEART
HT101 HEART 101 – PAGE 22
HT102 HEART 102 (BEATING) – PAGE 22
HT103 HEART 103 (ACHING) – PAGE 22
HT104 HEART 104 (JUMPING) – PAGE 23
HT105 HEART 105 (POUNDING) – PAGE 23
HT106 HEART 106 (STOPPING) – PAGE 25
HT107 HEART 107 (SINKING) – PAGE 25
HT108 HEART 108 (RACING) – PAGE 25
HT109 HEART 109 (SWELLING) – PAGE 25
HT110 HEART 110 (HEARTFELT JOY) – PAGE 25
HT111 HEART 111 (HEART FELT SORROW) – PAGE 26
HT112 HEART 112 (HARDENING HEART) – PAGE 26
HT113 HEART 113 (THINKING WITH THE HEART) – PAGE 26
HT114 HEART 114 (HEARING HEARTBEATS) – PAGE 26
HT115 HEART 115 (SKIPPING BEATS) – PAGE 27
HT116 HEART 116 (HEARTFELT FEAR) – PAGE 27
HT117 HEART 117 (FEELING HEARTBEAT) – PAGE 27
HT118 HEART 118 (PASSION) – PAGE 27
HT119 HEART 119 (CALMING) – PAGE 27

NERVES
NV101 NERVES 101 – PAGE 28
NV102 NERVES 102 (NERVE ENDINGS) – PAGE 30

PULSE
PL101 PULSE 101 – PAGE 30

BLOOD
BD101 BLOOD 101 – PAGE 32
BD102 BLOOD 102 (TURNING COLD) – PAGE 33
BD103 BLOOD 103 (BLEEDING) – PAGE 33

VEINS
VN101 VEINS 101 – PAGE 35
VN102 VEINS 102 (THROBBING) – PAGE 35

VN103 VEINS 103 (BULGING) – PAGE 36

BELLY
BL101 BELLY 101 - – PAGE 37
BL102 BELLY 102 (TOUCHING THE BELLY) – PAGE 37

STOMACH
ST101 STOMACH 101 (EMOTIONAL REACTIONS) – PAGE 37
ST102 STOMACH 102 (PHYSICAL SENSATIONS) – PAGE 38
ST103 STOMACH 103 (TOUCHING STOMACH) – PAGE 38

BOWELS
BW101 BOWELS 101 (SICK) – PAGE 39

HUNGER
HG101 HUNGER 101 – PAGE 39

WAIST
WT101 WAIST 101 – PAGE 40
WT102 WAIST 102 (SIDES) – PAGE 41
WT103 WAIST 103 (TOUCHING WAIST) – PAGE 41

BACK
BK101 BACK 101 – PAGE 42
BK102 BACK 102 (SPINE) – PAGE 42
BK103 BACK 103 (TOUCHING BACK) – PAGE 42
BK104 BACK 104 (FEELING SENSATIONS) – PAGE 43
BK105 BACK 105 (LYING ON BACK) – PAGE 43
BK106 BACK 106 (SUPPORTING BACK) – PAGE 44

BUTTOCKS
BT101 BUTTOCKS 101 – PAGE 44

HIPS
HP101 HIPS 101 – PAGE 44
HP102 HIPS 102 (MOVING HIPS) – PAGE 45
HP103 HIPS 103 (TOUCHING HIPS) – PAGE 45

ARMS
AR101 ARMS 101 – PAGE 46
AR102 ARMS 102 (HOLDING SOMEONE) – PAGE 47
AR103 ARMS 103 (HUGGING) – PAGE 49
AR104 ARMS 104 (RESTRAINING SOMEONE) – PAGE 50
AR105 ARMS 105 (CARRYING SOMETHING/SOMEONE) – PAGE 51
AR106 ARMS 106 (RAISING ARMS) – PAGE 52
AR107 ARMS 107 (LOWERING ARMS) – PAGE 52
AR108 ARMS 108 (MOVING ARMS) – PAGE 52

AR109 ARMS 109 (EMPTY) – PAGE 53
AR110 ARMS 110 (GESTURES) – PAGE 53
AR111 ARMS 111 (FOLDING) – PAGE 53
AR112 ARMS 112 (EXTRACTING FROM EMBRACE) – PAGE 54
AR113 ARMS 113 (SUPPORTING SOMETHING) – PAGE 54
AR114 ARMS 114 (FLEXING) – PAGE 54
AR115 ARMS 115 (STRAINING) – PAGE 54
AR116 ARMS 116 (ARMPITS) – PAGE 55

ELBOW
EB101 ELBOW 101 – PAGE 55
EB102 ELBOW 102 (SUPPORTING BODY) – PAGE 56

HANDS
HN101 HANDS 101 – PAGE 56
HN102 HANDS 102 (RAISING HANDS) – PAGE 59
HN103 HANDS 103 (LOWERING HANDS) – PAGE 60
HN104 HANDS 104 (MOVING HANDS) – PAGE 61
HN105 HANDS 105 (UNMOVING HANDS) – PAGE 61
HN106 HANDS 106 (FOLDED HANDS) – PAGE 61
HN107 HANDS 107 (FOLDING SOMETHING) – PAGE 62
HN108 HANDS 108 (WRINGING THE HANDS) – PAGE 62
HN109 HANDS 109 (TREMBLING HANDS) – PAGE 62
HN110 HANDS 110 (SLAPPING) – PAGE 62
HN111 HANDS 111 (PUSHING/PRESSING) – PAGE 63
HN112 HANDS 112 (PULLING) – PAGE 64
HN113 HANDS 113 (OPENING SOMETHING) – PAGE 66
HN114 HANDS 114 (CLOSING SOMETHING) – PAGE 66
HN115 HANDS 115 (HANDSHAKES) – PAGE 66
HN116 HANDS 116 (WAVING) – PAGE 66
HN117 HANDS 117 (GESTURES) – PAGE 67
HN118 HANDS 118 (TOUCHING) – PAGE 69
HN119 HANDS 119 (MASSAGE) – PAGE 74
HN120 HANDS 120 (WIPING) – PAGE 74
HN121 HANDS 121 (PATTING) – PAGE 75
HN122 HANDS 122 (CONCEALING SOMETHING) – PAGE 75
HN123 HANDS 123 (TOUCHING SEXUALLY) – PAGE 75
HN124 HANDS 124 (CARESSING) – PAGE 77
HN125 HANDS 125 (EXPLORATORY TOUCHING) – PAGE 56
HN126 HANDS 126 (RUBBING) – PAGE 80
HN127 HANDS 127 (HOLDING SOMEONE) – PAGE 81
HN128 HANDS 128 (RESTRAINING SOMEONE) – PAGE 83
HN129 HANDS 129 (HOLDING SOMETHING) – PAGE 85
HN130 HANDS 130 (POURING/SERVING) – PAGE 85
HN131 HANDS 131 (FISTS) – PAGE 86
HN132 HANDS 132 (PALMS) – PAGE 87
HN133 HANDS 133 (THROWING) – PAGE 88
HN134 HANDS 134(REACHING) – PAGE 89
HN135 HANDS 135 (WRITING/DRAWING) – PAGE 90

HN136 HANDS 136 (CLAPPING) – PAGE 90
HN137 HANDS 137 (HOLDING HANDS) – PAGE 90
HN138 HANDS 138 (COLD) – PAGE 91
HN139 HANDS 139 (TAKING/ACCEPTING SOMETHING) – PAGE 91
HN140 HANDS 140 (SETTING SOMETHING DOWN) – PAGE 92
HN141 HANDS 141 (PICKING SOMETHING UP) – PAGE 92
HN142 HANDS 142 (GIVING/OFFERING SOMETHING) – PAGE 92
HN143 HANDS 143 (LETTING GO/RELEASING) – PAGE 93
HN144 HANDS 144 (HITTING) – PAGE 93
HN145 HANDS 145 (SQUEEZING) – PAGE 94
HN146 HANDS 146 (NOT TOUCHING) – PAGE 94
HN147 HANDS 147 (AVOIDING RESTRAINT) – PAGE 94
HN148 HANDS 148 (SUPPORTING SOMETHING) – PAGE 95
HN149 HANDS 149 (CUPPING HANDS) – PAGE 95
HN150 HANDS 150 (GUIDING SOMEONE) – PAGE 96
HN151 HANDS 151 (SHAKING SOMEONE/SOMETHING) – PAGE 96
HN152 HANDS 152 (HANDS DANGLING) – PAGE 96
HN153 HANDS 153 (HANDS IN POCKETS) – PAGE 96
HN154 HANDS 154 (KISSING HAND) – PAGE 96
HN155 HANDS 155 (CLENCHING) – PAGE 97
HN156 HANDS 156 (UNCLENCHING) – PAGE 97
HN157 HANDS 157 (HANDS ON HIPS) – PAGE 97

WRIST
WR101 WRIST 101 – PAGE 97
WR102 WRIST 102 (MOVING) – PAGE 97
WR103 WRIST 103 (SENSATIONS) – PAGE 98
WR104 WRIST 104 (TOUCHING) – PAGE 98

FINGERS
FN101 FINGERS 101 – PAGE 99
FN102 FINGERS 102 (GRASPING) – PAGE 99
FN103 FINGERS 103 (TOUCHING) – PAGE 100
FN104 FINGERS 104 (TAPPING) – PAGE 102
FN105 FINGERS 105 (MOVING) – PAGE 102
FN106 FINGERS 106 (HOLDING) – PAGE 103
FN107 FINGERS 107 (GESTURING) – PAGE 103
FN108 FINGERS 108 (POKING) – PAGE 104
FN109 FINGERS 109 (GRIPPING) – PAGE 104
FN110 FINGERS 110 (KNUCKLES) – PAGE 105
FN111 FINGERS 111 (FINGER NAILS) – PAGE 105
FN112 FINGERS 112 (CHEWING NAILS) – PAGE 106
FN113 FINGERS 113 (THUMB) – PAGE 106
FN114 FINGERS 114 (POINTING) – PAGE 106
FN115 FINGERS 115 (FIDGETING) – PAGE 107
FN116 FINGERS 116 (SCRATCHING) – PAGE 107
FN117 FINGERS 117 (SNAPPING) – PAGE 107
FN118 FINGERS 118 (TRACING) – PAGE 107
FN119 FINGERS 119 (RUBBING) – PAGE 108

FN120 FINGERS 120 (SQUEEZING) – PAGE 108
FN121 FINGERS 121 (HOOKING WITH FINGER) – PAGE 109
FN122 FINGERS 122 (FEELING SENSATIONS) – PAGE 109
FN123 FINGERS 123 (OPENING SOMETHING) – PAGE 109
FN124 FINGERS 124 (PRESSING) – PAGE 109

LEGS
LG101 LEGS 101 – PAGE 110
LG102 LEGS 102 (LAP) – PAGE 110
LG103 LEGS 103 (CROSSING) – PAGE 110
LG104 LEGS 104 (SWINGING LEGS) – PAGE 111
LG105 LEGS 105 (STRETCHING LEGS) – PAGE 111
LG106 LEGS 106 (TOUCHING) – PAGE 111

THIGHS
TG101 THIGHS 101 – PAGE 112

KNEES
KN101 KNEES 101 – PAGE 113
KN102 KNEES 102 (TREMBLING) – PAGE 113
KN103 KNEES 103 (HOLDING KNEES) – PAGE 114
KN104 KNEES 104 (KNEELING) – PAGE 114
KN105 KNEES 105 (TOUCHING KNEES) – PAGE 115

CALVES
CV101 CALVES 101 – PAGE 115

ANKLES
AK101 ANKLES 101 – PAGE 116

FEET
FE101 FEET 101 – PAGE 117

TOES
TO101 TOES 101 – PAGE 118

MUSCLES
MU101 MUSCLES 101 – PAGE 119
MU102 MUSCLES 102 (WORKING) – PAGE 119
MU103 MUSCLES 103 (LOOSENING) – PAGE 119
MU104 MUSCLES 104 (TIGHTENING/FLINCHING) – PAGE 120
MU105 MUSCLES 105 (STIFF) – PAGE 120

BONES
BO101 BONES 101 – PAGE 121

BODY
BY101 BODY 101 – PAGE 123
BY102 BODY 102 (BODIES TOUCHING) – PAGE 123
BY103 BODIES TOUCHING (CHEST TO CHEST OR BREAST) – PAGE 127
BY104 BODY 104 (SENSATIONS) – PAGE 127

BODY MOVEMENT
BM101 BODY MOVEMENT 101 (KNEELING) – PAGE 128
BM102 BODY MOVEMENT 102 (TURNING) – PAGE 128
BM103 BODY MOVEMENT 103 (LEANING) – PAGE 131
BM104 BODY MOVEMENT 104 (STRETCHING) – PAGE 132
BM105 BODY MOVEMENT 105 (MOVING) – PAGE 133
BM106 BODY MOVEMENT 106 (SQUIRMING) – PAGE 134
BM107 BODY MOVEMENT 107 (BENDING) – PAGE 134
BM108 BODY MOVEMENT 108 (FOOTSTEPS) – PAGE 135
BM109 BODY MOVEMENT 109 (STEPPING) – PAGE 135
BM110 BODY MOVEMENT 110 (WALKING) – PAGE 136
BM111 BODY MOVEMENT 111 (WALKING TIPTOE) – PAGE 139
BM112 BODY MOVEMENT 112 (WALKING SLOWLY) – PAGE 139
BM113 BODY MOVEMENT 113 (WALKING PURPOSEFULLY) – PAGE 40
BM114 BODY MOVEMENT 114 (BACKING AWAY) – PAGE 140
BM115 BODY MOVEMENT 115 (PACING) – PAGE 141
BM116 BODY MOVEMENT 116 (RUNNING) – PAGE 141
BM117 BODY MOVEMENT 117 (CRAWLING) – PAGE 142
BM118 BODY MOVEMENT 118 (RISING) – PAGE 142
BM119 BODY MOVEMENT 119 (CLIMBING) – PAGE 145
BM120 BODY MOVEMENT 120 (DANCING) – PAGE 145
BM121 BODY MOVEMENT 121 (KICKING) – PAGE 145
BM122 BODY MOVEMENT 122 (JUMPING) – PAGE 146
BM123 BODY MOVEMENT 123 (SKIPPING) – PAGE 146
BM124 BODY MOVEMENT 124 (SWIMMING) – PAGE 146
BM125 BODY MOVEMENT 125 (FIGHTING) – PAGE 147
BM126 BODY MOVEMENT 126 (SHIVERING) – PAGE 148
BM127 BODY MOVEMENT 127 (TREMBLING) – PAGE 152
BM128 BODY MOVEMENT 128 (ROCKING) – PAGE 153
BM129 BODY MOVEMENT 129 (BOWING) – PAGE 153
BM130 BODY MOVEMENT 130 (CURTSYING) – PAGE 153
BM131 BODY MOVEMENT 131 (STRAIGHTENING) – PAGE 154
BM132 BODY MOVEMENT 132 (ADVANCING) – PAGE 154
BM133 BODY MOVEMENT 133 (APPROACHING SOMEONE) – PAGE 155
BM134 BODY MOVEMENT 134 (LEAVING) – PAGE 155
BM135 BODY MOVEMENT 135 (AVOIDING RESTRAINT) – PAGE 156
BM136 BODY MOVEMENT 136 (RESTRAINING SOMEONE) – PAGE 156
BM137 BODY MOVEMENT 137 (CURLING) – PAGE 157
BM138 BODY MOVEMENT 138 (FOLLOWING SOMEONE) – PAGE 157
BM139 BODY MOVEMENT 139 (SITTING UP) – PAGE 157
BM140 BODY MOVEMENT 140 (TRYING TO RISE) – PAGE 157
BM141 BODY MOVEMENT 141 (RE-ADJUSTING POSITION) – PAGE 158

BM142 BODY MOVEMENT 142 (MARCHING) – PAGE 158
BM143 BODY MOVEMENT 143 (SUPPORTING BODY) – PAGE 158

BODY STOPPING

BS101 BODY STOPPING 101 (UNABLE TO MOVE) – PAGE 158
BS102 BODY STOPPING 102 (STOPPING) – PAGE 159
BS103 BODY STOPPING 103 (NONE) – PAGE 159
BS104 BODY STOPPING 104 (STIFFENING) – PAGE 160
BS105 BODY STOPPING 105 (HIDING) – PAGE 161
BS106 BODY STOPPING 106 (COWERING) – PAGE 161
BS107 BODY STOPPING 107 (SLUMPING) – PAGE 161
BS108 BODY STOPPING 108 (LYING DOWN) – PAGE 161
BS109 BODY STOPPING 109 (THE PROCESS OF SITTING DOWN) – PAGE 161
BS110 BODY STOPPING 110 (FALLING) – PAGE 163 – PAGE 164
BS111 BODY IN MOTION 111 (STAGGER/STUMBLE)

BODY IN REPOSE

BIR101 BODY IN REPOSE 101 (LYING (ALONE) – PAGE 165
BIR102 BODY IN REPOSE 102 (LYING (WITH SOMEONE) – PAGE 165
BIR103 BODY IN REPOSE 103 (ALREADY SEATED POSITIONS) – PAGE 166
BIR104 BODY IN REPOSE 104 (STANDING) – PAGE 169
BIR105 BODY IN MOTION 105 (SQUATTING) – PAGE 170

DAILY ACTIVITIES
INDEX

DAILY ACTIVITIES

DAP101 USING A PHONE 101 (INITIATING A CALL) – PAGE 171
DAP102 USING A PHONE 102 (PHONE RINGING) – PAGE 171
DAP103 USING A PHONE 103 (ANSWERING PHONE) – PAGE 171
DAP104 USING A PHONE 104 (LISTENING TO CALLER) – PAGE 171
DAP105 USING A PHONE 105 (HOLDING PHONE) – PAGE 172
DAP106 USING A PHONE 106 (TERMINATING A CALL) – PAGE 172
DAC103 IN A CAR 103 (DRIVING A CAR) – PAGE 173
DAC104 IN A CAR 104 (ACCELERATING) – PAGE 173
DAC105 IN A CAR 105 (STOPPING) – PAGE 173
DAC106 IN A CAR 106 (ENTERING TRAFFIC) – PAGE 174
DAC107 IN A CAR 107 (DRIVING IN REVERSE) – PAGE 174
DAC108 IN A CAR 108I (LOOKING IN REARVIEW MIRROR) – PAGE 174
DAC109 IN A CAR 109 (CHANGING DIRECTION) – PAGE 174
DAC110 IN A CAR 110 (SLOWING DOWN) – PAGE 174
DAC111 IN A CAR 111 (PARKING) – PAGE 174
DAC112 IN A CAR 112 (GETTING OUT OF CAR) – PAGE 174
DAD101 DRESSING 101 (PUTTING ON CLOTHES) – PAGE 175
DAD102 DRESSING 102 (WEARING CLOTHES) – PAGE 175
DAD103 DRESSING 103 (TAKING OFF CLOTHES) – PAGE 176

DAD104 DRESSING 104 (CARRYING/WEARING A PURSE) – PAGE 178
DAD105 DRESSING 105 (LOOKING IN A MIRROR) – PAGE 178
DAD106 DRESSING 106 (PUTTING ON MAKEUP) – PAGE 178
DAD107 DRESSING 107 (APPLYING LOTION) – PAGE 178
DARW101 READING/WRITING 101 (WEARING GLASSES) – PAGE 179
DARW102 READING/WRITING 102 (READING) – PAGE 179
DARW103 READING/WRITING 103 (WRITING/DRAWING) – PAGE 179
DABS101 BATHING/SHOWERING 101 (BATHING/SHOWERING) – PAGE 179
DADWL101 DOORS/WINDOWS/LIGHTS 101 (TURNING LIGHTS ON/OFF) – PAGE 180
DADWL102 DOORS/WINDOWS/LIGHTS 102 (OPENING DOORS) – PAGE 180
DADWL103 DOORS/WINDOWS/LIGHTS 103 (CLOSING DOORS) – PAGE 181
DADWL104 DOORS/WINDOWS/LIGHTS 104 (KNOCKING ON DOOR) – PAGE 182
DADWL105 DOORS/WINDOWS/LIGHTS 105 (OPENING A WINDOW) – PAGE 182
DAED101 EATING/DRINKING 101 (COOKING) – PAGE 182
DAED102 EATING/DRINKING 102 (THE PROCESS OF DRINKING) – PAGE 182
DAED103 EATING/DRINKING 103 (THE PROCESS OF EATING) – PAGE 184
DAED104 EATING/DRINKING 104 (TOASTING) – PAGE 185
DASW101 SLEEPING/WAKING 101 (GOING TO SLEEP) – PAGE 185
DASW102 SLEEPING/WAKING 102 (SLEEPING) – PAGE 186
DASW103 SLEEPING/WAKING 103 (WAKING UP) – PAGE 186
DAH101 RIDING A HORSE 101 (RIDING A HORSE) – PAGE 187
DAS101 SMOKING 101 (SMOKING) – PAGE 189

FIGURES OF SPEECH INDEX

FS1 (FORCEFUL)

FS1-1 (TRUTHFUL) – PAGE 189
FS1-2 (FORCEFUL) – PAGE 189
FS1-3 (EXASPERATION) – PAGE 191
FS1-4 (UNWILLINGLY) – PAGE 191

FS2 (WISHFUL)

FS2-1 (WISHFUL) – PAGE 191
FS2-2 (WORRIED) – PAGE 192
FS2-3 (DESPERATION) – PAGE 192
FS2-4 (CAUTION) – PAGE 193

FS3 (QUESTIONING)

FS3-1 (TALKATIVE) – PAGE 193
FS3-2 (CONVERSATIONAL) – PAGE 193
FS3-3 (WONDERING) – PAGE 194
FS3-4 (COMPREHENDING) – PAGE 194
FS3-5 (QUESTIONING) – PAGE 194
FS3-6 (DOUBTFUL) – PAGE 195
FS3-7 (CONFUSED) – PAGE 195

FS3-8 (SARCASM) – PAGE 196
FS3-9 (ARGUMENTATIVE) – PAGE 196
FS3-10 (IRONY) – PAGE 197
FS3-11 (TESTY) – PAGE 198
FS3-12 (SHOCK) – PAGE 198
FS3-13 (INCOMPREHENSION) – PAGE 198

FS4 (NERVOUS)
FS4-1 (NERVOUS) – PAGE 199
FS4-2 (POLITENESS) – PAGE 200
FS4-3 (RELIEF) – PAGE 200
FS4-4 (TENSION) – PAGE 200
FS4-5 (SECRETIVE) – PAGE 201
FS4-6 (FEARFUL) – PAGE 201

FS5 (HUMOR)
FS5-1 (HUMOR) – PAGE 202
FS5-2 (HUMORING) – PAGE 203
FS5-3 (FUN) – PAGE 203
FS5-4 (LAUGHTER) – PAGE 203
FS5-5 (GRIMLY HUMOROUS) – PAGE 205

FS6 (SURPRISE)
FS6-1 (GUILT) – PAGE 205
FS6-2 (CONFUSION) – PAGE 205
FS6-3 (SURPRISE) – PAGE 205
FS6-4 (SHOCK) – PAGE 206

FS7 (A BREAK IN SPEECH)
FS7-1 (A PAUSE) – PAGE 207
FS7-2 (CONTINUATION) – PAGE 208
FS7-3 (CHANGING THE SUBJECT) – PAGE 210
FS7-4 (PURSUING THE SUBJECT FURTHER) – PAGE 210

FS8 (SOLEMNITY)
FS8-1 (SOLEMNITY) – PAGE 210
FS8-2 (APOLOGETIC) – PAGE 211
FS8-3 (PITY) – PAGE 211
FS8-4 (SADNESS) – PAGE 211
FS8-5 (CALMNESS) – PAGE 211
FS8-6 (CLEARLY UNDERSTOOD)

FS9 (DISCONTENT)
FS9-1 (APPROVAL) – PAGE 212
FS9-2 (CONTENT) – PAGE 212
FS9-3 (DISCONTENT) – PAGE 213

FS9-4 (INDIFFERENCE) – PAGE 214
FS9-5 (NEUTRAL) – PAGE 215

FS10 (COMMANDING)
FS10-1 (DIGNIFIED) – PAGE 215
FS10-2 (ASSURANCE) – PAGE 215
FS10-3 (COMMANDING) – PAGE 215
FS10-4 (AGREEMENT) – PAGE 216
FS10-5 (SUBSERVIENT) – PAGE 216

FS11 (PRIDE)
FS11-1 (PRIDE) – PAGE 217
FS11-2 (EMBARASSMENT) – PAGE 217

FS12 (HOPELESS)
FS12-1 (HURT) – PAGE 217
FS12-2 (SORROWFUL) – PAGE 217
FS12-3 (HOPELESSNESS) – PAGE 218
FS12-4 (TIREDLY) – PAGE 218
FS12-5 (DISAPPOINTMENT) – PAGE 219

FS13 (MALEVOLENT)
FS13-1 (MALEVOLENT) – PAGE 219
FS13-2 (DISGUST) – PAGE 220
FS13-3 (ANGER) – PAGE 220
FS13-4 (RUDE) – PAGE 222

FS14 (EXCITEMENT)
FS14-1 (EXCITEMENT) – PAGE 222
FS14-2 (SEXUAL EXCITEMENT) – PAGE225

FS15 (JOYFUL)
FS15-1 (FRIENDLY) – PAGE 225
FS15-2 (AFFECTION) – PAGE 226
FS15-3 (CONTENTEDNESS) – PAGE 226
FS15-4 (JOYFULL) – PAGE 226
FS15-5 (KINDNESS) – PAGE 227
FS15-6 (COMFORTING) – PAGE 227

FS16 (GREETINGS)
FS16-1 (GREETINGS) – PAGE 227
FS16-2 (SUMMONS) – PAGE 228
FS16-3 (FAREWELLS) – PAGE 228

EMOTIONS

INDEX

E1 (FORCEFUL)
E1-1 (TRUTHFUL) – PAGE 228
E1-2 (FORCEFUL) – PAGE 228
E1-3 (INTENSE) – PAGE 228

E2 (WISHFUL)
E2-1 (WISHFUL) – PAGE 229
E2-2 (WORRIED) – PAGE 229
E2-3 (DESPERATION) – PAGE 229
E2-4 (CAUTION) – PAGE 229

E3 (QUESTIONING)
E3-1 (WONDERING) – PAGE 229
E3-2 (QUESTIONING) – PAGE 229
E3-3 (DOUBTFUL) – PAGE 229
E3-4 (ARGUMENTATIVE) – PAGE 229

E4 (NERVOUS)
E4-1 (NERVOUS) – PAGE 230
E4-2 (FEARFUL) – PAGE 231
E4-3 (SELF-CONSCIOUS) – PAGE 231

E5 (HUMOR)
E5-1 (HUMOR) – PAGE 231

E6 (SURPRISE)
E6-1 (SURPRISE) – PAGE 231
E6-2 (SHOCK) – PAGE 232

E7 (SOLEMNITY)
E7-5 (CALMNESS) – PAGE 232

E8 (DISCONTENT)
E8-1 (PATIENT) – PAGE 232
E8-2 (DISCONTENT) – PAGE 232
E8-3 (INDIFFERENCE) – PAGE 233

E9 (COMMANDING)
E9-1 (DIGNIFIED) – PAGE 233
E9-2 (ASSURANCE) – PAGE 233
E9-3 (RESOLVE) – PAGE 233

E10 (PRIDE)
E10-1 (PRIDE) – PAGE 232

E10-2 (EMBARASSMENT) – PAGE 234

E11 (HOPELESS)
E11-1 (HOPELESSNESS) – PAGE 234
E11-2 (LONELINESS) – PAGE 235
E11-3 (MISERY) – PAGE 235

E12 (MALEVOLENT)
E12-1 (MALEVOLENT) – PAGE 235
E12-2 (ANGER) – PAGE 235

E13 (EXCITEMENT)
E13-1 (EXCITEMENT) – PAGE 235

E14 (JOYFUL)
E14-1 (AFFECTION) – PAGE 236
E14-2 (CONTENTEDNESS) – PAGE 236
E14-3 (JOYFULL) – PAGE 236
E14-4 (TRUST) – PAGE 237
E14-5 (LONGING/DESIRE) – PAGE 237

E15 (FEAR)
E15-1 (FEAR) – PAGE 237
E15-2 (PANIC) – PAGE 237

A note from Sybrina:

Once upon a time I wanted to be a writer more than anything in the world. I could tell stories with the best of them, so I just knew I could write well, too.

Funny thing about writing, though...it's nothing like telling a story. I bet you've noticed that, too. I'd even go as far as to bet there have been times...plenty of them, when you've been writing along just fine, then suddenly, you hit a brick wall over how to describe the simplest thing.

25 years ago, there wasn't anything much available other than Webster's Dictionary or Roget's Thesaurus and a couple of synonym and antonym books. So, I decided I'd start to put together what I was looking for, myself.

Those were the prehistoric days, before p.c.'s. Each bit of information I gathered was tediously placed behind index tabs in spiral notebooks...lots of notebooks and tons of tabs. It very quickly became a monstrous task. When I got my first computer, with Word Perfect's word "search and replace" features, I felt like I'd finally arrived in the 20th century but the best was yet to come. Word for Windows made cross-referencing all those phrases to all of their relevant categories a breeze.

Compiling this book has been a labor of love. Along the way, I have discovered my true writing skills lie, not in writing out my stories, but in organizing and categorizing information. Maybe someday, I'll actually have time to write my own great novel, but for now, I'm content in the knowledge that my work on Sybrina's Phrase Thesaurus has made it easier for other writers to get past their own brick walls. I hope you will enjoy reading the phrases in this tool as much as I have enjoyed compiling them.

Happy Writing! Visit www.sybrina.com to see other offerings.

Sybrina's Phrase Thesaurus Series

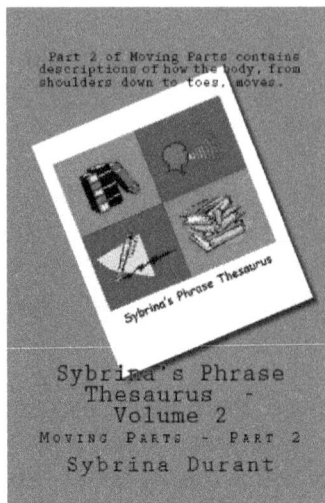

Part 1 of Moving Parts contains descriptions of how different elements of the head and face move.

Sybrina's Phrase Thesaurus - Volume 1
MOVING PARTS - PART 1
Sybrina Durant

Part 2 of Moving Parts contains descriptions of how the body, from shoulders down to toes, moves.

Sybrina's Phrase Thesaurus - Volume 2
MOVING PARTS - PART 2
Sybrina Durant

Volume 1
Moving Parts – Part 1

Volume 2
Moving Parts – Part 2

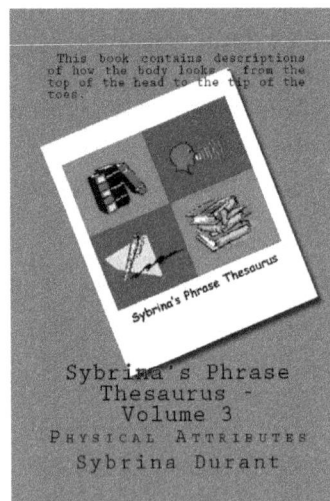

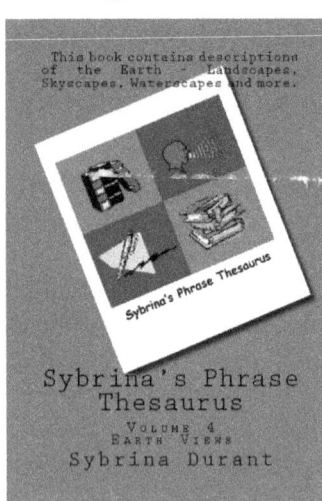

This book contains descriptions of how the body looks, from the top of the head to the tip of the toes.

Sybrina's Phrase Thesaurus - Volume 3
PHYSICAL ATTRIBUTES
Sybrina Durant

This book contains descriptions of the Earth - Landscapes, Skyscapes, Waterscapes and more.

Sybrina's Phrase Thesaurus
VOLUME 4
EARTH VIEWS
Sybrina Durant

Volume 3
Physical Attributes

Volume 4
Earth Views